The Ultimate
KETO DIET
Cookbook for Beginners

Over 1500 Days Flavorful and Satisfying Recipes to Say Goodbye to Weight Woes Eating Well and Living Well Every Day | 28 Day Meal Plan

Dorothy C. Schull

CONTENTS

INTRODUCTION I

What is Keto Diet?..I
How does the Keto Diet work?..I
What should Keto Diet eat?..II
Which food should be avoided in Keto Diet?.........................IV
Benefits of Keto Diet IV

28 Day Meal Plan VI

Measurement Conversions VIII

Appetizers, Snacks & Side Dishes Recipes.....................6

Buttery Herb Roasted Radishes 6
Jalapeno Popper Spread 6
Lemony Fried Artichokes 6
Baba Ganoush Eggplant Dip...7
Balsamic Brussels Sprouts With Prosciutto 7
Parmesan Crackers...8
Cheesy Chicken Fritters With Dill Dip 8
Simple Tender Crisp Cauli-bites...9
Party Bacon And Pistachio Balls 9
Spicy Devilled Eggs With Herbs 9
Mozzarella & Prosciutto Wraps 10
Stuffed Jalapeno 10
Roasted String Beans, Mushrooms & Tomato Plate...............10
Crispy Keto Pork Bites 11
Pesto Stuffed Mushrooms 11
Tart Raspberry Crumble Bar 12
Coconut And Chocolate Bars..12
Onion Cheese Muffins 13
Reese Cups...13
Garlic Flavored Kale Taters 13
Spinach And Ricotta Gnocchi..14
Teriyaki Chicken Wings 14
Balsamic Zucchini 15
Nutty Avocado Crostini With Nori...15
Devilled Eggs With Sriracha Mayo 16
Bacon-flavored Kale Chips..16

Poultry Recipes 17

Turkey, Coconut And Kale Chili 17
Pesto Chicken 17
Sweet Garlic Chicken Skewers 18
Chicken Thighs With Broccoli & Green Onions 18
Fried Chicken With Coconut Sauce 19
Roasted Chicken With Herbs 19
Chicken Country Style 19
Chili Turkey Patties With Cucumber Salsa 20
Chili Lime Chicken 20
Easy Asian Chicken 20
Oregano & Chili Flattened Chicken 21
Chicken Curry 21
Thyme Chicken Thighs 22
Roasted Chicken Breasts With Capers 22
Roast Chicken With Herb Stuffing 23
Smoky Paprika Chicken 23
Chicken With Monterey Jack Cheese 24
Chicken Breasts With Cheddar & Pepperoni 24
Chicken Gumbo 25
Roasted Chicken With Tarragon 25
Bacon And Chicken Cottage Pie 26
Turkey Enchilada Bowl 26
Chicken And Spinach 27
Simple Chicken Garlic-tomato Stew 27
Pancetta & Chicken Casserole 28
Cheese Stuffed Chicken Breasts With Spinach 28

Pork, Beef & Lamb Recipes 29

Peanut Butter Pork Stir-fry 29
Beef Brisket In Mustard Sauce 29
Mustardy Pork Chops 30
Beef Stovies 30
Simple Beef Curry 31
Beef Italian Sandwiches 31
Lemon Pork Chops With Buttered Brussels Sprouts 32
Simple Corned Beef 32
White Wine Lamb Chops 33
Pork Lettuce Cups 33
Ground Beef And Cabbage Stir Fry 33
Pancetta Sausage With Kale 34
Roasted Spicy Beef 34
Grilled Pork Loin Chops With Barbecue Sauce 35
Parsley Beef Burgers 35
Zoodle, Bacon, Spinach, And Halloumi Gratin 36

Beef And Ale Pot Roast 36
Pulled Pork With Avocado 37
Mushroom Pork Chops 37
Slow Cooker Pork 37
Spiced Pork Roast With Collard Greens 38
Jamaican Pork Oven Roast 38
Beef Enchilada Stew 38
Bacon Stew With Cauliflower 39
Pork Chops And Peppers 39
Beef Steak Filipino Style 39

Fish And Seafood Recipes 40

Steamed Chili-rubbed Tilapia 40
Baked Fish With Feta And Tomato 40
Lemon-rosemary Shrimps 40
Lemon Marinated Salmon With Spices 41
Blackened Fish Tacos With Slaw 41
Baked Salmon With Pistachio Crust 42
Golden Pompano In Microwave 42
Steamed Cod With Ginger 43
Shrimp Spread...43
Alaskan Cod With Mustard Cream Sauce 44
Enchilada Sauce On Mahi Mahi 44
Bacon Wrapped Salmon 44
Coconut Milk Sauce Over Crabs 45
Seasoned Salmon With Parmesan 45
Avocado And Salmon...45
Flounder With Dill And Capers 46
Shrimp In Curry Sauce..46
Salmon Panzanella 47
Cedar Salmon With Green Onion 47
Smoked Mackerel Patties...48
Angel Hair Shirataki With Creamy Shrimp 48
Cod With Balsamic Tomatoes 49
Thyme-sesame Crusted Halibut 49
Steamed Ginger Scallion Fish...49
Avocado Tuna Boats 50
Red Curry Halibut...50

Vegan, Vegetable & Meatless Recipes.. 51

Cauliflower Fritters 51
Creamy Cucumber Avocado Soup 51
Cauliflower & Hazelnut Salad 52
Vegetable Tempeh Kabobs...52
Brussels Sprouts With Tofu..53

Egg And Tomato Salad 53

Strawberry Mug Cake 53

Grilled Cauliflower 54

Tofu Sesame Skewers With Warm Kale Salad 54

Guacamole 55

Bell Pepper Stuffed Avocado 55

Grilled Spicy Eggplant...55

Garlic Lemon Mushrooms 56

Pumpkin Bake 56

Chard Swiss Dip 56

Grilled Cheese The Keto Way 57

Morning Coconut Smoothie 57

Cauliflower Mash 57

Grated Cauliflower With Seasoned Mayo 58

Cheesy Cauliflower Falafel 58

Cauliflower & Mushrooms Stuffed Peppers 59

Roasted Asparagus With Spicy Eggplant Dip 59

Paprika 'n Cajun Seasoned Onion Rings 60

Morning Granola 60

Zoodles With Avocado & Olives 61

Cauliflower Gouda Casserole 61

Soups, Stew & Salads Recipes 62

Citrusy Brussels Sprouts Salad 62

Chicken Cabbage Soup 62

Broccoli Slaw Salad With Mustard-mayo Dressing 62

Mexican Soup 63

Cobb Egg Salad In Lettuce Cups 63

Salsa Verde Chicken Soup 64

Homemade Cold Gazpacho Soup 64

Chicken And Cauliflower Rice Soup 65

Corn And Bacon Chowder 65

Sour Cream And Cucumbers 66

Balsamic Cucumber Salad 66

Creamy Cauliflower Soup With Chorizo Sausage 66

Tuna Caprese Salad..67

Crunchy And Salty Cucumber 67

Arugula Prawn Salad With Mayo Dressing 67

Insalata Caprese 68

Asparagus Niçoise Salad..68

Chicken Creamy Soup 68

Bacon And Pea Salad 69

Broccoli Cheese Soup 69

Butternut And Kale Soup 70

Minty Watermelon Cucumber 70

Coconut Cauliflower Soup 70
Easy Tomato Salad 71
Bacon Tomato Salad 71
Watermelon And Cucumber Salad 71

Desserts And Drinks Recipes 72

Strawberry Yogurt Shake 72
Vanilla Bean Frappuccino 72
Nutritiously Green Milk Shake 72
Vanilla Flan With Mint 73
Granny Smith Apple Tart 73
Coconut-melon Yogurt Shake 74
Boysenberry And Greens Shake 74
No Nuts Fudge 74
Brownies With Coco Milk 75
Eggless Strawberry Mousse 75
Coffee Fat Bombs 75
Green Tea Brownies With Macadamia Nuts 76
Lemon Gummies 76
Spicy Cheese Crackers 77
Coco-loco Creamy Shake 77
Green And Fruity Smoothie 77
Almond Milk Hot Chocolate 78
Coconut Milk Pudding 78
Blackberry Cheese Vanilla Blocks 78
Choco Coffee Milk Shake 79
Creamy Choco Shake 79
Crispy Zucchini Chips 79
Cardamom-cinnamon Spiced Coco-latte 80
Nutty Arugula Yogurt Smoothie 80
Chocolate Cakes 81
Cranberry White Chocolate Barks 81

Appendix : Recipes Index 82

INTRODUCTION

Introducing Dorothy C. Schull's "Ultimate Keto Diet Cookbook" - a culinary journey designed to sculpt your physique while tantalizing your taste buds! As a passionate food lover and nutrition expert, Dorothy brings the magic of her kitchen to yours, transforming the seemingly daunting ketogenic diet into an exciting and accessible wellness adventure.

Her unique approach demystifies the science behind the Keto Diet, merging nutritional facts with culinary flair. Dorothy believes that the journey to well-being doesn't have to mean bland meals. Instead, she encourages a celebration of rich, bold flavors that will have you falling in love with each bite.

Every page of her cookbook paints a vibrant picture of Dorothy's passion for health and taste, offering over 1000 delicious, easy-to-follow recipes tailored to fit the Keto lifestyle. From hearty breakfasts to indulgent desserts, Dorothy covers every craving, ensuring you never feel deprived on your path to optimal health.

If you thought Keto was just about bacon and cheese, think again. With Dorothy's guidance, explore a new universe of culinary possibilities that promote weight loss, energy boost, improved focus, and more. Get ready to embark on a delicious journey with Dorothy C. Schull's "Ultimate Keto Diet Cookbook." Your transformation begins in the kitchen!

What is Keto Diet?

The Keto Diet, short for "ketogenic diet," is a high-fat, moderate-protein, and very low-carbohydrate eating plan. Its primary aim is to shift the body's metabolism from burning carbohydrates as its main source of energy to burning fats, a state known as ketosis. When the body enters ketosis, it starts converting stored fats into ketones, which then serve as a primary energy source. Advocates of the diet tout benefits ranging from weight loss, enhanced mental clarity, sustained energy, and improved blood sugar levels. The significant reduction in carbs intake means that foods like bread, pasta, and sugary treats are replaced with fats from avocados, nuts, oils, and meats.

How does the Keto Diet work?

Carbohydrate reduction: The basic principle of the ketogenic diet is to reduce the intake of carbohydrates, usually less than 50 grams per day. This drastic reduction causes the body to use up glucose, its main fuel source from carbohydrates.

Enter Ketosis: With the consumption of glucose, the body begins to break down the fat stored in the liver to produce ketone bodies. This metabolic state in which the body primarily burns fat for energy while the brain uses ketones for fuel is called ketosis.

Fat as main fuel: In ketosis, due to the limited supply of glucose, the body becomes very efficient at burning fat for energy. This diet also resulted in significantly lower insulin levels, which further caused the fat cells to release more fat.

Maintain Muscle Mass: Although your overall calorie intake decreases when you start a ketogenic diet, moderate protein intake can help maintain muscle mass. Ketones are also muscle protective, meaning they prevent protein (the protein that makes up muscle) from being broken down for energy.

Appetite regulation: Ketone bodies have an inhibitory effect on appetite. In addition, fats and proteins are known to satiate more than carbohydrates, thereby reducing hunger and thus reducing calorie intake naturally.

Stabilize Blood Sugar: Without regular carbohydrate intake, blood sugar levels tend to stabilize, reducing the highs and lows that often occur with high-carb diets.

Essentially, a keto diet promotes the burning of stored fat for energy by mimicking the body's response to starvation without actually starving for food. This metabolic adaptation not only aids in weight loss, but may also lead to other health benefits, such as improved mental clarity, energy levels and metabolic function.

What should Keto Diet eat?

The Keto Diet emphasizes foods that are high in healthy fats, moderate in protein, and very low in carbohydrates. Here's a list of foods that those on a Keto Diet typically eat:

1. **Fats and Oils:**

   - Healthy fats are the cornerstone of the keto diet. This includes:

     - Avocado and avocado oil

     - Olive oil, coconut oil, MCT oil, and butter or ghee

     - Lard and tallow from pasture-raised animals

     - Nuts and seeds like almonds, chia seeds, flaxseeds, and macadamia

2. **Proteins:**

   - Meat and poultry: Grass-fed beef, pork, lamb, chicken, and turkey.

   - Fish: Fatty fish like salmon, mackerel, sardines, and trout.

   - Eggs: Preferably pasture-raised or organic.

   - Full-fat dairy: Cheese, cream, butter, and Greek or natural yogurt (in moderation).

3. Vegetables:

- Low-carb veggies: Spinach, kale, lettuce, broccoli, cauliflower, Brussels sprouts, asparagus, and zucchini.

- Remember to always consider the net carbs (total carbs minus fiber) of the vegetable.

4. Dairy:

- Since milk has a higher carb count due to lactose (a sugar), it's consumed in limited quantities. Instead, focus on high-fat dairy like heavy cream, butter, and hard cheeses.

5. Nuts and Seeds:

- In moderation: Almonds, walnuts, flaxseeds, chia seeds, and macadamia nuts are among the most keto-friendly.

6. Beverages:

- Water (still or sparkling) should be your primary beverage.

- Herbal teas and bone broth are also good choices.

- Coffee and tea are acceptable but try to limit the amount of caffeine.

- If alcohol is consumed, it should be spirits that are low in carbs like vodka or gin, but in moderation.

7. Condiments:

- Mustard, mayonnaise (without added sugar), hot sauces, and herbs and spices are generally okay. Always read labels for hidden sugars or unhealthy fats.

8. Snacks:

- Cheese, olives, pork rinds, nuts, and seeds can be consumed as snacks.

III

Which food should be avoided in Keto Diet?

In the Keto Diet, the primary goal is to minimize carbohydrate intake so that the body enters a metabolic state called ketosis, where it burns fat for energy. Given this, here are the foods and ingredients that should generally be avoided or limited:

• **Sugary Foods and Drinks**

Sodas, fruit juices, smoothies, cake, ice cream, candy, etc.

Most fruits, except small portions of berries like strawberries.

• **Grains and Starches**

Wheat-based products: Bread, pasta, rice, cereals, etc.

Grains like barley, oats, and corn.

• **Legumes**

Beans, lentils, chickpeas, and peas.

• **Root Vegetables and Tubers**

Potatoes, sweet potatoes, carrots, and parsnips.

• **Some Dairy**

Milk (due to its sugar content) and low-fat dairy products which often have added sugars.

• **Unhealthy Fats**

Processed vegetable oils (like canola, soybean, and sunflower oil) and margarine.

Trans fats, which are found in processed foods with the term "hydrogenated" on the ingredients list.

• **Alcohol**

Many alcoholic beverages contain carbs. If you do consume, opt for spirits with no mixers or low-carb options and drink in moderation.

• **Sugary Sauces and Condiments**

Barbecue sauce, ketchup (unless sugar-free), and some salad dressings can be high in sugar and carbs.

• **Diet or Low-Fat Products**

These are often high in sugar and processed to replace the fat content.

• **Sugar-Free Diet Foods**

These can be high in sugar alcohols, which can affect ketone levels in some people. They can also be processed and may contain other non-keto ingredients.

Benefits of Keto Diet

Weight Loss

The Keto Diet helps the body enter ketosis, where it starts burning fat as its primary energy source, often resulting in weight loss. This diet also helps reduce hunger-stimulating hormones, making you feel satiated longer.

Improved Blood Sugar and Insulin Levels

Many studies have shown that the Keto Diet can be effective in stabilizing blood sugar levels and can be beneficial for those with type 2 diabetes.

Enhanced Brain Function

The ketones produced during ketosis can provide an alternative fuel for the brain. Some people report improved concentration, clarity, and cognitive function while on the Keto Diet.

Increased Energy

Once the body adjusts to ketosis, many people experience a consistent energy level throughout the day, with fewer energy crashes compared to carb-heavy diets.

Heart Health

The Keto Diet can lead to a reduction in cholesterol levels, particularly LDL (bad cholesterol) and triglycerides. At the same time, it can increase HDL (good cholesterol) levels.

Appetite Control

Fat is incredibly satiating. With a higher fat intake on the Keto Diet, many people experience reduced appetite, leading to a natural reduction in calorie intake.

Supports Metabolic Syndrome Management

Metabolic syndrome, a cluster of conditions like high blood pressure, insulin resistance, and abdominal obesity, can be managed better with the Keto Diet.

Mood Stabilization

Some people report a reduction in mood swings, and there's growing interest in studying the Keto Diet's potential benefits for certain mental health conditions.

Might Reduce Inflammation

Lowering carb intake can reduce the markers of inflammation in the body. Chronic inflammation is linked to several chronic diseases.

Improved Skin Health

Some individuals notice a reduction in acne and other skin issues on the Keto Diet, potentially due to the reduction in insulin levels and inflammation.

28 Day Meal Plan

Day	Breakfast	Lunch	Dinner
1	Balsamic Brussels Sprouts With Prosciutto 7	Turkey, Coconut And Kale Chili 17	Chili Turkey Patties With Cucumber Salsa 20
2	Parmesan Crackers 8	Pesto Chicken 17	Cauliflower Fritters 51
3	Cheesy Chicken Fritters With Dill Dip 8	Sweet Garlic Chicken Skewers 18	Creamy Cucumber Avocado Soup 51
4	Party Bacon And Pistachio Balls 9	Chicken Thighs With Broccoli & Green Onions 18	Cauliflower & Hazelnut Salad 52
5	Spicy Devilled Eggs With Herbs 9	Fried Chicken With Coconut Sauce 19	Vegetable Tempeh Kabobs 52
6	Mozzarella & Prosciutto Wraps 10	Roasted Chicken With Herbs 19	Brussels Sprouts With Tofu 53
7	Pesto Stuffed Mushrooms 11	Chicken Country Style 19	Egg And Tomato Salad 53
8	Tart Raspberry Crumble Bar 12	Chili Lime Chicken 20	Grilled Cauliflower 54
9	Coconut And Chocolate Bars 12	Easy Asian Chicken 20	Tofu Sesame Skewers With Warm Kale Salad 54
10	Onion Cheese Muffins 13	Oregano & Chili Flattened Chicken 21	Guacamole 55
11	Spinach And Ricotta Gnocchi 14	Chicken Curry 21	Bell Pepper Stuffed Avocado 55
12	Devilled Eggs With Sriracha Mayo 16	Thyme Chicken Thighs 22	Grilled Spicy Eggplant 55
13	Chicken Gumbo 25	Roasted Chicken Breasts With Capers 22	Garlic Lemon Mushrooms 56
14	Bacon And Chicken Cottage Pie 26	Roast Chicken With Herb Stuffing 23	Grilled Cheese The Keto Way 57

Day	Breakfast	Lunch	Dinner
15	Strawberry Mug Cake 53	Smoky Paprika Chicken 23	Cauliflower Mash 57
16	Pumpkin Bake 56	Chicken With Monterey Jack Cheese 24	Grated Cauliflower With Seasoned Mayo 58
17	Morning Coconut Smoothie 57	Chicken Breasts With Cheddar & Pepperoni 24	Cheesy Cauliflower Falafel 58
18	Morning Granola 60	Roasted Chicken With Tarragon 25	Cauliflower & Mushrooms Stuffed Peppers 59
19	Corn And Bacon Chowder 65	Turkey Enchilada Bowl 26	Roasted Asparagus With Spicy Eggplant Dip 59
20	Balsamic Cucumber Salad 66	Chicken And Spinach 27	Paprika 'n Cajun Seasoned Onion Rings 60
21	Creamy Cauliflower Soup With Chorizo Sausage 66	Simple Chicken Garlic-tomato Stew 27	Zoodles With Avocado & Olives 61
22	Tuna Caprese Salad 67	Pancetta & Chicken Casserole 28	Cauliflower Gouda Casserole 61
23	Arugula Prawn Salad With Mayo Dressing 67	Cheese Stuffed Chicken Breasts With Spinach 28	Citrusy Brussels Sprouts Salad 62
24	Bacon And Pea Salad 69	Peanut Butter Pork Stir-fry 29	Chicken Cabbage Soup 62
25	Granny Smith Apple Tart 73	Beef Brisket In Mustard Sauce 29	Mexican Soup 63
26	Coconut-melon Yogurt Shake 74	Mustardy Pork Chops 30	Cobb Egg Salad In Lettuce Cups 63
27	Boysenberry And Greens Shake 74	Beef Stovies 30	Salsa Verde Chicken Soup 64
28	Brownies With Coco Milk 75	Simple Beef Curry 31	Homemade Cold Gazpacho Soup 64

Measurement Conversions

BASIC KITCHEN CONVERSIONS & EQUIVALENTS

DRY MEASUREMENTS CONVERSION CHART

3 TEASPOONS = 1 TABLESPOON = 1/16 CUP

6 TEASPOONS = 2 TABLESPOONS = 1/8 CUP

12 TEASPOONS = 4 TABLESPOONS = 1/4 CUP

24 TEASPOONS = 8 TABLESPOONS = 1/2 CUP

36 TEASPOONS = 12 TABLESPOONS = 3/4 CUP

48 TEASPOONS = 16 TABLESPOONS = 1 CUP

METRIC TO US COOKING CONVERSIONS

OVEN TEMPERATURES

120 °C = 250 °F

160 °C = 320 °F

180° C = 350 °F

205 °C = 400 °F

220 °C = 425 °F

LIQUID MEASUREMENTS CONVERSION CHART

8 FLUID OUNCES = 1 CUP = 1/2 PINT = 1/4 QUART

16 FLUID OUNCES = 2 CUPS = 1 PINT = 1/2 QUART

32 FLUID OUNCES = 4 CUPS = 2 PINTS = 1 QUART

 = 1/4 GALLON

128 FLUID OUNCES = 16 CUPS = 8 PINTS = 4 QUARTS = 1 GALLON

BAKING IN GRAMS

1 CUP FLOUR = 140 GRAMS

1 CUP SUGAR = 150 GRAMS

1 CUP POWDERED SUGAR = 160 GRAMS

1 CUP HEAVY CREAM = 235 GRAMS

VOLUME

1 MILLILITER = 1/5 TEASPOON

5 ML = 1 TEASPOON

15 ML = 1 TABLESPOON

240 ML = 1 CUP OR 8 FLUID OUNCES

1 LITER = 34 FL. OUNCES

WEIGHT

1 GRAM = .035 OUNCES

100 GRAMS = 3.5 OUNCES

500 GRAMS = 1.1 POUNDS

1 KILOGRAM = 35 OUNCES

US TO METRIC COOKING CONVERSIONS

1/5 TSP = 1 ML

1 TSP = 5 ML

1 TBSP = 15 ML

1 FL OUNCE = 30 ML

1 CUP = 237 ML

1 PINT (2 CUPS) = 473 ML

1 QUART (4 CUPS) = .95 LITER

1 GALLON (16 CUPS) = 3.8 LITERS

1 OZ = 28 GRAMS

1 POUND = 454 GRAMS

BUTTER

1 CUP BUTTER = 2 STICKS = 8 OUNCES = 230 GRAMS = 8 TABLESPOONS

WHAT DOES 1 CUP EQUAL

1 CUP = 8 FLUID OUNCES

1 CUP = 16 TABLESPOONS

1 CUP = 48 TEASPOONS

1 CUP = 1/2 PINT

1 CUP = 1/4 QUART

1 CUP = 1/16 GALLON

1 CUP = 240 ML

BAKING PAN CONVERSIONS

1 CUP ALL-PURPOSE FLOUR = 4.5 OZ

1 CUP ROLLED OATS = 3 OZ 1 LARGE EGG = 1.7 OZ

1 CUP BUTTER = 8 OZ 1 CUP MILK = 8 OZ

1 CUP HEAVY CREAM = 8.4 OZ

1 CUP GRANULATED SUGAR = 7.1 OZ

1 CUP PACKED BROWN SUGAR = 7.75 OZ

1 CUP VEGETABLE OIL = 7.7 OZ

1 CUP UNSIFTED POWDERED SUGAR = 4.4 OZ

BAKING PAN CONVERSIONS

9-INCH ROUND CAKE PAN = 12 CUPS

10-INCH TUBE PAN =16 CUPS

11-INCH BUNDT PAN = 12 CUPS

9-INCH SPRINGFORM PAN = 10 CUPS

9 X 5 INCH LOAF PAN = 8 CUPS

9-INCH SQUARE PAN = 8 CUPS

Appetizers, Snacks & Side Dishes Recipes

Buttery Herb Roasted Radishes

Servings: 6
Cooking Time: 25 Minutes
Ingredients:

- 2 lb small radishes, greens removed
- 3 tbsp olive oil
- Salt and black pepper to season
- 3 tbsp unsalted butter
- 1 tbsp chopped parsley
- 1 tbsp chopped tarragon

Directions:

1. Preheat oven to 400ºF and line a baking sheet with parchment paper. Toss radishes with oil, salt, and black pepper. Spread on baking sheet and roast for 20 minutes until browned.
2. Heat butter in a large skillet over medium heat to brown and attain a nutty aroma, 2 to 3 minutes.
3. Take out the parsnips from the oven and transfer to a serving plate. Pour over the browned butter atop and sprinkle with parsley and tarragon. Serve with roasted rosemary chicken.

Nutrition Info:

- Info Per Servings 2g Carbs, 5g Protein, 14g Fat, 160 Calories

Jalapeno Popper Spread

Servings: 8
Cooking Time: 3 Mins
Ingredients:

- 2 packages cream cheese, softened; low-carb
- 1 cup. mayonnaise
- 1 can chopped green chilies, drained
- 2 ounces canned diced jalapeno peppers, drained
- 1 cup. grated Parmesan cheese

Directions:

1. Combine cream cheese and mayonnaise in a bowl until incorporated. Add in jalapeno peppers and green chilies. In a microwave safe bowl, spread jalapeno peppers mixture and sprinkle with Parmesan cheese.
2. Microwave jalapeno peppers mixture on High about 3 minutes or until warm.

Nutrition Info:

- Info Per Servings 1g Carbs, 2.1g Protein, 11.1g Fat, 110 Calories

Lemony Fried Artichokes

Servings: 4
Cooking Time: 20 Minutes
Ingredients:

- 12 fresh baby artichokes
- 2 tbsp lemon juice
- 2 tbsp olive oil
- Salt to taste

Directions:

1. Slice the artichokes vertically into narrow wedges. Drain on paper towels before frying.
2. Heat olive oil in a cast-iron skillet over high heat. Fry the artichokes until browned and crispy. Drain excess oil on paper towels. Sprinkle with salt and lemon juice.

Nutrition Info:

- Info Per Servings 2.9g Carbs, 2g Protein, 2.4g Fat, 35 Calories

Baba Ganoush Eggplant Dip

Servings: 4

Cooking Time: 80 Minutes

Ingredients:

- 1 head of garlic, unpeeled
- 1 large eggplant, cut in half lengthwise
- 5 tablespoons olive oil
- Lemon juice to taste
- 2 minced garlic cloves
- What you'll need from the store cupboard:
- Pepper and salt to taste

Directions:

1. With the rack in the middle position, preheat oven to 350°F.
2. Line a baking sheet with parchment paper. Place the eggplant cut side down on the baking sheet.
3. Roast until the flesh is very tender and pulls away easily from the skin, about 1 hour depending on the eggplant's size. Let it cool.
4. Meanwhile, cut the tips off the garlic cloves. Place the cloves in a square of aluminum foil. Fold up the edges of the foil and crimp together to form a tightly sealed packet. Roast alongside the eggplant until tender, about 20 minutes. Let cool.
5. Mash the cloves by pressing with a fork.
6. With a spoon, scoop the flesh from the eggplant and place it in the bowl of a food processor. Add the mashed garlic, oil and lemon juice. Process until smooth. Season with pepper.

Nutrition Info:

- Info Per Servings 10.2g Carbs, 1.6g Protein, 17.8g Fat, 192 Calories

Balsamic Brussels Sprouts With Prosciutto

Servings: 4

Cooking Time: 40 Minutes

Ingredients:

- 3 tbsp balsamic vinegar
- 1 tbsp erythritol
- ½ tbsp olive oil
- Salt and black pepper to taste
- 1 lb Brussels sprouts, halved
- 5 slices prosciutto, chopped

Directions:

1. Preheat oven to 400ºF and line a baking sheet with parchment paper. Mix balsamic vinegar, erythritol, olive oil, salt, and black pepper and combine with the brussels sprouts in a bowl.
2. Spread the mixture on the baking sheet and roast for 30 minutes until tender on the inside and crispy on the outside. Toss with prosciutto, share among 4 plates, and serve with chicken breasts.

Nutrition Info:

- Info Per Servings 0g Carbs, 8g Protein, 14g Fat, 166 Calories

Parmesan Crackers

Servings: 6
Cooking Time: 25 Minutes
Ingredients:
- 1 ⅓ cups coconut flour
- 1 ¼ cup grated Parmesan cheese
- Salt and black pepper to taste
- 1 tsp garlic powder
- ⅓ cup butter, softened
- ⅓ tsp sweet paprika
- ⅓ cup heavy cream
- Water as needed

Directions:
1. Preheat the oven to 350ºF.
2. Mix the coconut flour, parmesan cheese, salt, pepper, garlic powder, and paprika in a bowl. Add in the butter and mix well. Top with the heavy cream and mix again until a smooth, thick mixture has formed. Add 1 to 2 tablespoon of water at this point, if it is too thick.
3. Place the dough on a cutting board and cover with plastic wrap. Use a rolling pin to spread out the dough into a light rectangle. Cut cracker squares out of the dough and arrange them on a baking sheet without overlapping. Bake for 20 minutes and transfer to a serving bowl after.

Nutrition Info:
- Info Per Servings 0.7g Carbs, 5g Protein, 3g Fat, 115 Calories

Cheesy Chicken Fritters With Dill Dip

Servings: 4
Cooking Time: 40 Minutes + Cooling Time
Ingredients:
- 1 lb chicken breasts, thinly sliced
- 1 ¼ cup mayonnaise
- ¼ cup coconut flour
- 2 eggs
- Salt and black pepper to taste
- 1 cup grated mozzarella cheese
- 4 tbsp chopped dill
- 3 tbsp olive oil
- 1 cup sour cream
- 1 tsp garlic powder
- 1 tbsp chopped parsley
- 2 tbsp finely chopped onion

Directions:
1. In a bowl, mix 1 cup of the mayonnaise, 3 tbsp of dill, sour cream, garlic powder, onion, and salt. Cover the bowl with plastic wrap and refrigerate for 30 minutes.
2. Mix the chicken, remaining mayonnaise, coconut flour, eggs, salt, pepper, mozzarella, and remaining dill, in a bowl. Cover the bowl with plastic wrap and refrigerate it for 2 hours. After the marinating time is over, remove from the fridge.
3. Place a skillet over medium fire and heat the olive oil. Fetch 2 tablespoons of chicken mixture into the skillet, use the back of a spatula to flatten the top. Cook for 4 minutes, flip, and fry for 4 more.
4. Remove onto a wire rack and repeat the cooking process until the batter is finished, adding more oil as needed. Garnish the fritters with parsley and serve with dill dip.

Nutrition Info:
- Info Per Servings 0.8g Carbs, 12g Protein, 7g Fat, 151 Calories

Simple Tender Crisp Cauli-bites

Servings: 3

Cooking Time: 10 Minutes

Ingredients:

- 2 cups cauliflower florets
- 2 clove garlic minced
- 4 tablespoons olive oil
- ¼ tsp salt
- ½ tsp pepper

Directions:

1. In a small bowl, mix well olive oil salt, pepper, and garlic.
2. Place cauliflower florets on a baking pan. Drizzle with seasoned oil and toss well to coat.
3. Evenly spread in a single layer and place a pan on the top rack of the oven.
4. Broil on low for 5 minutes. Turnover florets and return to the oven.
5. Continue cooking for another 5 minutes.
6. Serve and enjoy.

Nutrition Info:

- Info Per Servings 4.9g Carbs, 1.7g Protein, 18g Fat, 183 Calories

Party Bacon And Pistachio Balls

Servings: 8

Cooking Time: 45 Minutes

Ingredients:

- 8 bacon slices, cooked and chopped
- 8 ounces Liverwurst
- ¼ cup chopped pistachios
- 1 tsp Dijon mustard
- 6 ounces cream cheese

Directions:

1. Combine the liverwurst and pistachios in the bowl of your food processor. Pulse until smooth. Whisk the cream cheese and mustard in another bowl. Make 12 balls out of the liverwurst mixture.
2. Make a thin cream cheese layer over. Coat with bacon, arrange on a plate and chill for 30 minutes.

Nutrition Info:

- Info Per Servings 1.5g Carbs, 7g Protein, 12g Fat, 145 Calories

Spicy Devilled Eggs With Herbs

Servings: 4

Cooking Time: 30 Minutes

Ingredients:

- 12 large eggs
- 1 ½ cups water
- 6 tbsp mayonnaise
- Salt and chili pepper to taste
- 1 tsp mixed dried herbs
- ½ tsp sugar-free Worcestershire sauce
- ¼ tsp Dijon mustard
- A pinch of sweet paprika
- Chopped parsley to garnish
- Ice water Bath

Directions:

1. Pour the water into a saucepan, add the eggs, and bring to boil on high heat for 10 minutes. Cut the eggs in half lengthways and remove the yolks into a medium bowl. Use a fork to crush the yolks.
2. Add the mayonnaise, salt, chili pepper, dried herbs, Worcestershire sauce, mustard, and paprika. Mix together until a smooth paste has formed. Then, spoon the mixture into the piping bag and fill the egg white holes with it. Garnish with the chopped parsley and serve immediately.

Nutrition Info:

- Info Per Servings 0.4g Carbs, 6.7g Protein, 9.3g Fat, 112 Calories

Mozzarella & Prosciutto Wraps

Servings: 6
Cooking Time: 15 Minutes
Ingredients:

- 6 thin prosciutto slices
- 18 basil leaves
- 18 mozzarella ciliegine

Directions:

1. Cut the prosciutto slices into three strips. Place basil leaves at the end of each strip. Top with mozzarella. Wrap the mozzarella in prosciutto. Secure with toothpicks.

Nutrition Info:

- Info Per Servings 0.1g Carbs, 13g Protein, 12g Fat, 163 Calories

Stuffed Jalapeno

Servings: 4
Cooking Time: 20 Minutes
Ingredients:

- 12 jalapeno peppers, halved lengthwise and seeded
- 2-oz cream cheese softened
- 2-oz shredded cheddar cheese
- ¼ cup almond meal
- Salt and pepper to taste

Directions:

1. Spray a cookie sheet with cooking spray and preheat oven to 400oF.
2. Equally fill each jalapeno with cheddar cheese, cream cheese, and sprinkle almond meal on top. Place on a prepped baking sheet.
3. Pop in oven and bake for 20 minutes.
4. Serve and enjoy.

Nutrition Info:

- Info Per Servings 7.7g Carbs, 5.9g Protein, 13.2g Fat, 187 Calories

Roasted String Beans, Mushrooms & Tomato Plate

Servings: 4
Cooking Time: 32 Minutes
Ingredients:

- 2 cups strings beans, cut in halves
- 1 lb cremini mushrooms, quartered
- 3 tomatoes, quartered
- 2 cloves garlic, minced
- 3 tbsp olive oil
- 3 shallots, julienned
- ½ tsp dried thyme
- Salt and black pepper to season

Directions:

1. Preheat oven to 450ºF. In a bowl, mix the strings beans, mushrooms, tomatoes, garlic, olive oil, shallots, thyme, salt, and pepper. Pour the vegetables in a baking sheet and spread them all around.
2. Place the baking sheet in the oven and bake the veggies for 20 to 25 minutes.

Nutrition Info:

- Info Per Servings 6g Carbs, 6g Protein, 2g Fat, 121 Calories

Crispy Keto Pork Bites

Servings: 3
Cooking Time: 30 Minutes
Ingredients:
- ½ pork belly, sliced to thin strips
- 1 tablespoon butter
- 1 onion, diced
- 4 tablespoons coconut cream
- Salt and pepper to taste

Directions:
1. Place all ingredients in a mixing bowl and allow to marinate in the fridge for 2 hours.
2. When 2 hours is nearly up, preheat oven to 400oF and lightly grease a cookie sheet with cooking spray.
3. Place the pork strips in an even layer on the cookie sheet.
4. Roast for 30 minutes and turnover halfway through cooking.

Nutrition Info:
- Info Per Servings 1.9g Carbs, 19.1g Protein, 40.6g Fat, 448 Calories

Pesto Stuffed Mushrooms

Servings: 6
Cooking Time: 25 Minutes
Ingredients:
- 6 large cremini mushrooms
- 6 bacon slices
- 2 tablespoons basil pesto
- 5 tablespoons low-fat cream cheese softened

Directions:
1. Line a cookie sheet with foil and preheat oven to 375oF.
2. In a small bowl mix well, pesto and cream cheese.
3. Remove stems of mushrooms and discard. Evenly fill mushroom caps with pesto-cream cheese filling.
4. Get one stuffed mushroom and a slice of bacon. Wrap the bacon all over the mushrooms. Repeat process on remaining mushrooms and bacon.
5. Place bacon-wrapped mushrooms on prepared pan and bake for 25 minutes or until bacon is crispy.
6. Let it cool, evenly divide into suggested servings, and enjoy.

Nutrition Info:
- Info Per Servings 2.0g Carbs, 5.0g Protein, 12.2g Fat, 137.8 Calories

Tart Raspberry Crumble Bar

Servings: 9

Cooking Time: 55 Minutes

Ingredients:

- 1/2 cup whole toasted almonds
- 1 cup almond flour
- 1 cup cold, unsalted butter, cut into cubes
- 2 eggs, beaten
- 3-ounce dried raspberries
- 1/4 teaspoon salt
- 3 tbsp MCT or coconut oil.

Directions:

1. In a food processor, pulse almonds until chopped coarsely. Transfer to a bowl.

2. Add almond flour and salt into the food processor and pulse until a bit combined. Add butter, eggs, and MCT oil. Pulse until you have a coarse batter. Evenly divide batter into two bowls.

3. In the first bowl of batter, knead well until it forms a ball. Wrap in cling wrap, flatten a bit and chill for an hour for easy handling.

4. In the second bowl of batter, add the raspberries. In a pinching motion, pinch batter to form clusters of streusel. Set aside.

5. When ready to bake, preheat oven to 375oF and lightly grease an 8x8-inch baking pan with cooking spray.

6. Discard cling wrap and evenly press dough on the bottom of the pan, up to 1-inch up the sides of the pan, making sure that everything is covered in dough.

7. Top with streusel.

8. Pop in the oven and bake until golden brown and berries are bubbly around 45 minutes.

9. Remove from oven and cool for 20 minutes before slicing into 9 equal bars.

10. Serve and enjoy or store in a lidded container for 10-days in the fridge.

Nutrition Info:

- Info Per Servings 3.9g Carbs, 2.8g Protein, 22.9g Fat, 229 Calories

Coconut And Chocolate Bars

Servings: 6

Cooking Time: 30 Minutes

Ingredients:

- 1 tbsp Stevia
- ¾ cup shredded coconut, unsweetened
- ½ cup ground nuts (almonds, pecans, or walnuts)
- ¼ cup unsweetened cocoa powder
- 4 tbsp coconut oil
- Done

Directions:

1. In a medium bowl, mix shredded coconut, nuts, and cocoa powder.

2. Add Stevia and coconut oil.

3. Mix batter thoroughly.

4. In a 9x9 square inch pan or dish, press the batter and for a 30-minutes place in the freezer.

5. Serve and enjoy.

Nutrition Info:

- Info Per Servings 2.3g Carbs, 1.6g Protein, 17.8g Fat, 200 Calories

Onion Cheese Muffins

Servings: 6
Cooking Time: 20 Minutes
Ingredients:

- ¼ cup Colby jack cheese, shredded
- ¼ cup shallots, minced
- 1 cup almond flour
- 1 egg
- 3 tbsp sour cream
- ½ tsp salt
- 3 tbsp melted butter or oil

Directions:

1. Line 6 muffin tins with 6 muffin liners. Set aside and preheat oven to 350oF.
2. In a bowl, stir the dry and wet ingredients alternately. Mix well using a spatula until the consistency of the mixture becomes even.
3. Scoop a spoonful of the batter to the prepared muffin tins.
4. Bake for 20 minutes in the oven until golden brown.
5. Serve and enjoy.

Nutrition Info:

- Info Per Servings 4.6g Carbs, 6.3g Protein, 17.4g Fat, 193 Calories

Reese Cups

Servings: 12
Cooking Time: 1 Minute
Ingredients:

- ¼ cup unsweetened shredded coconut
- 1 cup almond butter
- ½ cup dark chocolate chips
- 1 tablespoon Stevia
- 1 tablespoon coconut oil

Directions:

1. Line 12 muffin tins with 12 muffin liners.
2. Place the almond butter, honey, and oil in a glass bowl and microwave for 30 seconds or until melted. Divide the mixture into 12 muffin tins. Let it cool for 30 minutes in the fridge.
3. Add the shredded coconuts and mix until evenly distributed.
4. Pour the remaining melted chocolate on top of the coconuts. Freeze for an hour.
5. Carefully remove the chocolates from the muffin tins to create perfect Reese cups.
6. Serve and enjoy.

Nutrition Info:

- Info Per Servings 10.7g Carbs, 5.0g Protein, 17.1g Fat, 214 Calories

Garlic Flavored Kale Taters

Servings: 4
Cooking Time: 20 Minutes
Ingredients:

- 4 cups kale, rinsed and chopped
- 2 cups cauliflower florets, finely chopped
- 2 tbsp almond milk
- 1 clove of garlic, minced
- 3 tablespoons oil
- 1/8 teaspoon black pepper
- cooking spray

Directions:

1. Heat oil in a large skillet and sauté the garlic for 2 minutes. Add the kale until it wilts. Transfer to a large bowl.
2. Add the almond milk. Season with pepper to taste.
3. Evenly divide into 4 and form patties.
4. Lightly grease a baking pan with cooking spray. Place patties on pan. Place pan on the top rack of the oven and broil on low for 6 minutes. Turnover patties and cook for another 4 minutes.
5. Serve and enjoy.

Nutrition Info:

- Info Per Servings 5g Carbs, 2g Protein, 11g Fat, 117 Calories

Spinach And Ricotta Gnocchi

Servings: 4
Cooking Time: 13 Minutes
Ingredients:
- 3 cups chopped spinach
- 1 cup ricotta cheese
- 1 cup Parmesan cheese , grated
- ¼ tsp nutmeg powder
- 1 egg, cracked into a bowl
- Salt and black pepper
- Almond flour, on standby
- 2 ½ cups water
- 2 tbsp butter

Directions:
1. To a bowl, add the ricotta cheese, half of the parmesan cheese, egg, nutmeg powder, salt, spinach, almond flour, and pepper. Mix well. Make quenelles of the mixture using 2 tbsp and set aside.
2. Bring the water to boil over high heat on a stovetop, about 5 minutes. Place one gnocchi onto the water, if it breaks apart; add some more flour to the other gnocchi to firm it up.
3. Put the remaining gnocchi in the water to poach and rise to the top, about 2 minutes. Remove the gnocchi with a perforated spoon to a serving plate.
4. Melt the butter in a microwave and pour over the gnocchi. Sprinkle with the remaining parmesan cheese and serve with a green salad.

Nutrition Info:
- Info Per Servings 4.1g Carbs, 6.5g Protein, 8.3g Fat, 125 Calories

Teriyaki Chicken Wings

Servings: 9
Cooking Time: 50 Minutes
Ingredients:
- 3 pounds chicken wings
- 1 onion, chopped
- 2 cups commercial teriyaki sauce
- 1 tablespoon chili garlic paste
- 2 teaspoons ginger paste
- Salt and pepper to taste

Directions:
1. In a heavy-bottomed pot, place on medium-high fire and lightly grease with cooking spray.
2. Pan fry chicken for 4 minutes per side. Cook in two batches.
3. Stir in remaining ingredients in a pot, along with the chicken.
4. Cover and cook on low fire for 30 minutes, stirring every now and then. Continue cooking until desired sauce thickness is achieved.
5. Serve and enjoy.

Nutrition Info:
- Info Per Servings 5.4g Carbs, 34.3g Protein, 5.4g Fat, 214 Calories

Balsamic Zucchini

Servings: 4

Cooking Time: 20 Minutes

Ingredients:

- 3 medium zucchinis, cut into thin slices
- 1/2 cup chopped sweet onion
- 1/2 teaspoon dried rosemary, crushed
- 2 tablespoons balsamic vinegar
- 1/3 cup crumbled feta cheese
- 1/2 teaspoon salt
- 1/4 teaspoon pepper
- 4 tablespoon olive oil

Directions:

1. In a large skillet, heat oil over medium-high heat; sauté zucchini and onion until crisp-tender, 6-8 minutes. Stir in seasonings. Add vinegar; cook and stir 2 minutes. Top with cheese.

Nutrition Info:

- Info Per Servings 5g Carbs, 4g Protein, 16g Fat, 175 Calories

Nutty Avocado Crostini With Nori

Servings: 4

Cooking Time: 12 Minutes

Ingredients:

- 8 slices low carb baguette
- 4 nori sheets
- 1 cup mashed avocado
- ⅓ tsp salt
- 1 tsp lemon juice
- 1 ½ tbsp coconut oil
- ⅓ cup chopped raw walnuts
- 1 tbsp chia seeds

Directions:

1. In a bowl, flake the nori sheets into the smallest possible pieces.
2. In another bowl, mix the avocado, salt, and lemon juice, and stir in half of the nori flakes. Set aside.
3. Place the baguette on a baking sheet and toast in a broiler on medium heat for 2 minutes, making sure not to burn. Remove the crostini after and brush with coconut oil on both sides.
4. Top each crostini with the avocado mixture and garnish with the chia seeds, chopped walnuts, Serve the snack immediately.

Nutrition Info:

- Info Per Servings 2.8g Carbs, 13.7g Protein, 12.2g Fat, 195 Calories

Devilled Eggs With Sriracha Mayo

Servings: 4
Cooking Time: 15 Minutes
Ingredients:

- 8 large eggs
- 3 cups water
- Ice water bath
- 3 tbsp sriracha sauce
- 4 tbsp mayonnaise
- Salt to taste
- ¼ tsp smoked paprika

Directions:

1. Bring eggs to boil in salted water in a pot over high heat, and then reduce the heat to simmer for 10 minutes. Transfer eggs to an ice water bath, let cool completely and peel the shells.
2. Slice the eggs in half height wise and empty the yolks into a bowl. Smash with a fork and mix in sriracha sauce, mayonnaise, and half of the paprika until smooth.
3. Spoon filling into a piping bag with a round nozzle and fill the egg whites to be slightly above the brim. Garnish with remaining paprika and serve immediately.

Nutrition Info:

- Info Per Servings 1g Carbs, 4g Protein, 19g Fat, 195 Calories

Bacon-flavored Kale Chips

Servings: 6
Cooking Time: 25 Minutes
Ingredients:

- 2 tbsp butter
- ¼ cup bacon grease
- 1-lb kale, around 1 bunch
- 1 to 2 tsp salt

Directions:

1. Remove the rib from kale leaves and tear it into 2-inch pieces.
2. Clean the kale leaves thoroughly and dry them inside a salad spinner.
3. In a skillet, add the butter to the bacon grease and warm the two fats under low heat. Add salt and stir constantly.
4. Set aside and let it cool.
5. Put the dried kale in a Ziploc back and add the cool liquid bacon grease and butter mixture.
6. Seal the Ziploc back and gently shake the kale leaves with the butter mixture. The leaves should have this shiny consistency, which means that they are coated evenly with the fat.
7. Pour the kale leaves on a cookie sheet and sprinkle more salt if necessary.
8. Bake for 25 minutes inside a preheated 350oF oven or until the leaves start to turn brown as well as crispy.

Nutrition Info:

- Info Per Servings 6.6g Carbs, 3.3g Protein, 13.1g Fat, 148 Calories

Poultry Recipes

Turkey, Coconut And Kale Chili

Servings: 5
Cooking Time: 30 Minutes
Ingredients:
- 18 ounces turkey breasts, cubed
- 1 cup kale, chopped
- 20 ounces canned diced tomatoes
- 2 tbsp coconut oil
- 2 tbsp coconut cream
- 2 garlic cloves, peeled and minced
- 2 onions, and sliced
- 1 tbsp ground coriander
- 2 tbsp fresh ginger, grated
- 1 tbsp turmeric
- 1 tbsp cumin
- Salt and ground black pepper, to taste
- 2 tbsp chili powder

Directions:
1. Set a pan over medium-high heat and warm the coconut oil, stir in the turkey and onion, and cook for 5 minutes. Place in garlic and ginger, and cook for 1 minute. Stir in the tomatoes, pepper, turmeric, coriander, salt, cumin, and chili powder. Place in the coconut cream, and cook for 10 minutes.
2. Transfer to an immersion blender alongside kale; blend well. Allow simmering, cook for 15 minutes.

Nutrition Info:
- Info Per Servings 4.2g Carbs, 25g Protein, 15.2g Fat, 295 Calories

Pesto Chicken

Servings: 4
Cooking Time: 30 Minutes
Ingredients:
- 2 cups basil leaves
- ¼ cup + 1 tbsp extra virgin olive oil, divided
- 5 sun-dried tomatoes
- 4 chicken breasts
- 6 cloves garlic, smashed, peeled, and minced
- What you'll need from the store cupboard:
- Salt and pepper to taste
- Water

Directions:
1. Put in the food processor the basil leaves, ¼ cup olive oil, and tomatoes. Season with salt and pepper to taste. Add a cup of water if needed.
2. Season chicken breasts with pepper and salt generously.
3. On medium fire, heat a saucepan for 2 minutes. Add a tbsp of olive oil to the pan and swirl to coat bottom and sides. Heat oil for a minute.
4. Add chicken and sear for 5 minutes per side.
5. Add pesto sauce, cover, and cook on low fire for 15 minutes or until chicken is cooked thoroughly.
6. Serve and enjoy.

Nutrition Info:
- Info Per Servings 1.1g Carbs, 60.8g Protein, 32.7g Fat, 556 Calories

Sweet Garlic Chicken Skewers

Servings: 4

Cooking Time: 17 Minutes + Time Refrigeration

Ingredients:

- For the Skewers
- 3 tbsp soy sauce
- 1 tbsp ginger-garlic paste
- 2 tbsp swerve brown sugar
- Chili pepper to taste
- 2 tbsp olive oil
- 3 chicken breasts, cut into cubes
- For the Dressing
- ½ cup tahini
- ½ tsp garlic powder
- Pink salt to taste
- ¼ cup warm water

Directions:

1. In a small bowl, whisk the soy sauce, ginger-garlic paste, brown sugar, chili pepper, and olive oil.
2. Put the chicken in a zipper bag, pour the marinade over, seal and shake for an even coat. Marinate in the fridge for 2 hours.
3. Preheat a grill to 400ºF and thread the chicken on skewers. Cook for 10 minutes in total with three to four turnings to be golden brown. Plate them. Mix the tahini, garlic powder, salt, and warm water in a bowl. Pour into serving jars.
4. Serve the chicken skewers and tahini dressing with cauli fried rice.

Nutrition Info:

- Info Per Servings 2g Carbs, 15g Protein, 17.4g Fat, 225 Calories

Chicken Thighs With Broccoli & Green Onions

Servings: 2

Cooking Time: 25 Minutes

Ingredients:

- 2 chicken thighs, skinless, boneless, cut into strips
- 1 tbsp olive oil
- 1 tsp red pepper flakes
- 1 tsp onion powder
- 1 tbsp fresh ginger, grated
- ¼ cup tamari sauce
- ½ tsp garlic powder
- ½ cup water
- ½ cup erythritol
- ½ tsp xanthan gum
- ½ cup green onions, chopped
- 1 small head broccoli, cut into florets

Directions:

1. Set a pan over medium heat and warm oil, cook in the chicken and ginger for 4 minutes. Stir in the water, onion powder, pepper flakes, garlic powder, tamari sauce, xanthan gum, and erythritol, and cook for 15 minutes. Add in the green onions and broccoli, cook for 6 minutes. Serve hot.

Nutrition Info:

- Info Per Servings 5g Carbs, 27g Protein, 23g Fat, 387 Calories

Fried Chicken With Coconut Sauce

Servings: 6

Cooking Time: 35 Minutes

Ingredients:

- 1 tbsp coconut oil
- 3 ½ pounds chicken breasts
- 1 cup chicken stock
- 1¼ cups leeks, chopped
- 1 tbsp lime juice
- ¼ cup coconut cream
- 2 tsp paprika
- 1 tsp red pepper flakes
- 2 tbsp green onions, chopped
- Salt and ground black pepper, to taste

Directions:

1. Set a pan over medium-high heat and warm oil, place in the chicken, cook each side for 2 minutes, set to a plate, and set aside. Set heat to medium, place the leeks to the pan and cook for 4 minutes.

2. Stir in the pepper, stock, pepper flakes, salt, paprika, coconut cream, and lime juice. Take the chicken back to the pan, place in more pepper and salt, cook while covered for 15 minutes.

Nutrition Info:

- Info Per Servings 3.2g Carbs, 58g Protein, 35g Fat, 491 Calories

Roasted Chicken With Herbs

Servings: 12

Cooking Time: 50 Minutes

Ingredients:

- 1 whole chicken
- ½ tsp onion powder
- ½ tsp garlic powder
- Salt and black pepper, to taste
- 2 tbsp olive oil
- 1 tsp dry thyme
- 1 tsp dry rosemary
- 1 ½ cups chicken broth
- 2 tsp guar gum

Directions:

1. Rub the chicken with half of the oil, salt, rosemary, thyme, pepper, garlic powder, and onion powder. Place the rest of the oil into a baking dish, and add chicken. Place in the stock, and bake for 40 minutes. Remove the chicken to a platter, and set aside. Stir in the guar gum in a pan over medium heat, and cook until thickening. Place sauce over chicken to serve.

Nutrition Info:

- Info Per Servings 1.1g Carbs, 33g Protein, 15g Fat, 367 Calories

Chicken Country Style

Servings: 4

Cooking Time: 25 Minutes

Ingredients:

- 3 tablespoons butter
- 1 packet dry Lipton's onion soup mix
- 1 can Campbell's chicken gravy
- 4 skinless and boneless chicken breasts
- 1/3 teaspoon pepper
- 1 cup water

Directions:

1. Add all ingredients in a pot on high fire and bring it to a boil.
2. Once boiling, lower fire to a simmer and cook for 25 minutes.
3. Adjust seasoning to taste.
4. Serve and enjoy.

Nutrition Info:

- Info Per Servings 6.8g Carbs, 53.7g Protein, 16.9g Fat, 380 Calories

Chili Turkey Patties With Cucumber Salsa

Servings: 4
Cooking Time: 30 Minutes
Ingredients:

- 2 spring onions, thinly sliced
- 1 pound ground turkey
- 1 egg
- 2 garlic cloves, minced
- 1 tbsp chopped herbs
- 1 small chili pepper, deseeded and diced
- 2 tbsp ghee
- Cucumber Salsa
- 1 tbsp apple cider vinegar
- 1 tbsp chopped dill
- 1 garlic clove, minced
- 2 cucumbers, grated
- 1 cup sour cream
- 1 jalapeño pepper, minced
- 2 tbsp olive oil

Directions:

1. Place all turkey ingredients, except the ghee, in a bowl. Mix to combine. Make patties out of the mixture. Melt the ghee in a skillet over medium heat. Cook the patties for 3 minutes per side.
2. Place all salsa ingredients in a bowl and mix to combine. Serve the patties topped with salsa.

Nutrition Info:

- Info Per Servings 5g Carbs, 26g Protein, 38g Fat, 475 Calories

Chili Lime Chicken

Servings: 5
Cooking Time: 30 Minutes
Ingredients:

- 1 lb. chicken breasts, skin and bones removed
- Juice from 1 ½ limes, freshly squeezed
- 1 tbsp. chili powder
- 1 tsp. cumin
- 6 cloves garlic, minced
- Pepper and salt to taste
- 1 cup water
- 4 tablespoon olive oil

Directions:

1. Place all ingredients in a heavy-bottomed pot and give a good stir.
2. Place on high fire and bring it to a boil. Cover, lower fire to a simmer, and cook for 20 minutes.
3. Remove chicken and place in a bowl. Shred using two forks. Return shredded chicken to the pot.
4. Boil for 10 minutes or until sauce is rendered.
5. Serve and enjoy.

Nutrition Info:

- Info Per Servings 1.5g Carbs, 19.3g Protein, 19.5g Fat, 265 Calories

Easy Asian Chicken

Servings: 5
Cooking Time: 16 Minutes
Ingredients:

- 1 ½ lb. boneless chicken breasts, sliced into strips
- 1 tbsp ginger slices
- 3 tbsp coconut aminos
- ¼ cup organic chicken broth
- 3 cloves of garlic, minced
- 5 tablespoons sesame oil

Directions:

1. On high fire, heat a heavy-bottomed pot for 2 minutes. Add oil to a pan and swirl to coat bottom and sides. Heat oil for a minute.
2. Add garlic and ginger sauté for a minute.
3. Stir in chicken breast and sauté for 5 minutes. Season with coconut aminos and sauté for another 2 minutes.
4. Add remaining ingredients and bring to a boil.
5. Let it boil for 5 minutes.
6. Serve and enjoy.

Nutrition Info:

- Info Per Servings 1.2g Carbs, 30.9g Protein, 17.6g Fat, 299 Calories

Oregano & Chili Flattened Chicken

Servings: 6

Cooking Time: 5 Minutes

Ingredients:

- 6 chicken breasts
- 4 cloves garlic, minced
- ½ cup oregano leaves, chopped
- ½ cup lemon juice
- 2/3 cup olive oil
- ¼ cup erythritol
- Salt and black pepper to taste
- 3 small chilies, minced

Directions:

1. Preheat a grill to 350°F.
2. In a bowl, mix the garlic, oregano, lemon Juice, olive oil, and erythritol. Set aside.
3. While the spices incorporate in flavor, cover the chicken with plastic wraps, and use the rolling pin to pound to ½ -inch thickness. Remove the wrap afterward, and brush the mixture on the chicken on both sides. Place on the grill, cover the lid and cook for 15 minutes.
4. Then, baste the chicken with more of the spice mixture, and continue cooking for 15 more minutes.

Nutrition Info:

- Info Per Servings 3g Carbs, 26g Protein, 9g Fat, 265 Calories

Chicken Curry

Servings: 6

Cooking Time: 30 Minutes

Ingredients:

- 1 ½ lb. boneless chicken breasts
- 2 tbsp. curry powder
- 2 cups chopped tomatoes
- 2 cups coconut milk, freshly squeezed
- 1 thumb-size ginger, peeled and sliced
- Pepper and salt to taste
- 2 tsp oil, divided

Directions:

1. On high fire, heat a saucepan for 2 minutes. Add 1 tsp oil to the pan and swirl to coat bottom and sides. Heat oil for a minute.
2. Sear chicken breasts for 4 minutes per side. Transfer to a chopping board and chop into bite-sized pieces.
3. Meanwhile, in the same pan, add remaining oil and heat for a minute. Add ginger sauté for a minute. Stir in tomatoes and curry powder. Crumble and wilt tomatoes for 5 minutes.
4. Add chopped chicken and continue sautéing for 7 minutes.
5. Deglaze the pot with 1 cup of coconut milk. Season with pepper and salt. Cover and simmer for 15 minutes.
6. Stir in remaining coconut milk and cook until heated through, around 3 minutes.

Nutrition Info:

- Info Per Servings 7.4g Carbs, 28.1g Protein, 22.4g Fat, 336 Calories

Thyme Chicken Thighs

Servings: 4
Cooking Time: 30 Minutes
Ingredients:

- ½ cup chicken stock
- 1 tbsp olive oil
- ½ cup chopped onion
- 4 chicken thighs
- ¼ cup heavy cream
- 2 tbsp Dijon mustard
- 1 tsp thyme
- 1 tsp garlic powder

Directions:

1. Heat the olive oil in a pan. Cook the chicken for about 4 minutes per side. Set aside. Sauté the onion in the same pan for 3 minutes, add the stock, and simmer for 5 minutes. Stir in mustard and heavy cream, along with thyme and garlic powder. Pour the sauce over the chicken and serve.

Nutrition Info:

- Info Per Servings 4g Carbs, 33g Protein, 42g Fat, 528 Calories

Roasted Chicken Breasts With Capers

Servings: 6
Cooking Time: 65 Minutes
Ingredients:

- 3 medium lemons, sliced
- ½ tsp salt
- 1 tsp olive oil
- 3 chicken breasts, halved
- Salt and black pepper to season
- ¼ cup almond flour
- 2 tsp olive oil
- 2 tbsp capers, rinsed
- 1 ¼ cup chicken broth
- 2 tsp butter
- 1 ½ tbsp chopped fresh parsley
- Parsley for garnish

Directions:

1. Preheat the oven to 350ºF and then lay a piece of parchment paper on a baking sheet.
2. Lay the lemon slices on the baking sheet, drizzle them with olive oil and sprinkle with salt. Roast in the oven for 25 minutes to brown the lemon rinds.
3. Cover the chicken halves with plastic wrap, place them on a flat surface, and gently pound with the rolling pin to flatten to about ½ -inch thickness. Remove the plastic wraps and season the chicken with salt and pepper.
4. Next, dredge the chicken in the almond flour on each side, and shake off any excess flour. Set aside.
5. Heat the olive oil in a skillet over medium heat and fry the chicken on both sides to a golden brown, for about 8 minutes in total. Then, pour the chicken broth in, shake the skillet, and let the broth boil and reduce to a thick consistency, about 12 minutes.
6. Lightly stir in the capers, roasted lemon, pepper, butter, and parsley, and simmer on low heat for 10 minutes. Turn the heat off and serve the chicken with the sauce hot, an extra garnish of parsley with a creamy squash mash.

Nutrition Info:

- Info Per Servings 3g Carbs, 33g Protein, 23g Fat, 430 Calories

Roast Chicken With Herb Stuffing

Servings: 8

Cooking Time: 120 Minutes

Ingredients:

- 5-pound whole chicken
- 1 bunch oregano
- 1 bunch thyme
- 1 tbsp marjoram
- 1 tbsp parsley
- 1 tbsp olive oil
- 2 pounds Brussels sprouts
- 1 lemon
- 4 tbsp butter

Directions:

1. Preheat your oven to 450°F.
2. Stuff the chicken with oregano, thyme, and lemon. Make sure the wings are tucked over and behind.
3. Roast for 15 minutes. Reduce the heat to 325°F and cook for 40 minutes. Spread the butter over the chicken, and sprinkle parsley and marjoram. Add the brussels sprouts. Return to the oven and bake for 40 more minutes. Let sit for 10 minutes before carving.

Nutrition Info:

- Info Per Servings 5.1g Carbs, 30g Protein, 32g Fat, 432 Calories

Smoky Paprika Chicken

Servings: 8

Cooking Time: 10 Minutes

Ingredients:

- 2 lb. chicken breasts, sliced into strips
- 2 tbsp. smoked paprika
- 1 tsp Cajun seasoning
- 1 tbsp minced garlic
- 1 large onion, sliced thinly
- Salt and pepper to taste
- 1 tbsp. olive oil

Directions:

1. In a large bowl, marinate chicken strips in paprika, Cajun, pepper, salt, and minced garlic for at least 30 minutes.
2. On high fire, heat a saucepan for 2 minutes. Add oil to the pan and swirl to coat bottom and sides. Heat oil for a minute.
3. Stir fry chicken and onion for 7 minutes or until chicken is cooked.
4. Serve and enjoy.

Nutrition Info:

- Info Per Servings 1.5g Carbs, 34g Protein, 12.4g Fat, 217 Calories

Chicken With Monterey Jack Cheese

Servings: 3
Cooking Time: 30 Minutes
Ingredients:

- 2 tbsp butter
- 1 tsp garlic, minced
- 1 pound chicken breasts
- 1 tsp creole seasoning
- ¼ cup scallions, chopped
- ½ cup tomatoes, chopped
- ½ cup chicken stock
- ¼ cup whipping cream
- ½ cup Monterey Jack cheese, grated
- ¼ cup fresh cilantro, chopped
- Salt and black pepper, to taste
- 4 ounces cream cheese
- 8 eggs
- A pinch of garlic powder

Directions:

1. Set a pan over medium heat and warm 1 tbsp butter. Add chicken, season with creole seasoning and cook each side for 2 minutes; remove to a plate. Melt the rest of the butter and stir in garlic and tomatoes; cook for 4 minutes. Return the chicken to the pan and pour in stock; cook for 15 minutes. Place in whipping cream, scallions, salt, Monterey Jack cheese, and pepper; cook for 2 minutes.

2. In a blender, combine the cream cheese with garlic powder, salt, eggs, and pepper, and pulse well. Place the mixture into a lined baking sheet, and then bake for 10 minutes in the oven at 325ºF. Allow the cheese sheet to cool down, place on a cutting board, roll, and slice into medium slices. Split the slices among bowls and top with chicken mixture. Sprinkle with chopped cilantro to serve.

Nutrition Info:

- Info Per Servings 4g Carbs, 39g Protein, 34g Fat, 445 Calories

Chicken Breasts With Cheddar & Pepperoni

Servings: 4
Cooking Time: 40 Minutes
Ingredients:

- 12 oz canned tomato sauce
- 1 tbsp olive oil
- 4 chicken breast halves, skinless and boneless
- Salt and ground black pepper, to taste
- 1 tsp dried oregano
- 4 oz cheddar cheese, sliced
- 1 tsp garlic powder
- 2 oz pepperoni, sliced

Directions:

1. Preheat your oven to 390ºF. Using a bowl, combine chicken with oregano, salt, garlic, and pepper.

2. Heat a pan with the olive oil over medium-high heat, add in the chicken, cook each side for 2 minutes, and remove to a baking dish. Top with the cheddar cheese slices spread the sauce, then cover with pepperoni slices. Bake for 30 minutes. Serve warm garnished with fresh oregano if desired

Nutrition Info:

- Info Per Servings 4.5g Carbs, 32g Protein, 21g Fat, 387 Calories

Chicken Gumbo

Servings: 5
Cooking Time: 40 Minutes
Ingredients:

- 2 sausages, sliced
- 3 chicken breasts, cubed
- 1 cup celery, chopped
- 2 tbsp dried oregano
- 2 bell peppers, seeded and chopped
- 1 onion, peeled and chopped
- 2 cups tomatoes, chopped
- 4 cups chicken broth
- 3 tbsp dried thyme
- 2 tbsp garlic powder
- 2 tbsp dry mustard
- 1 tsp cayenne powder
- 1 tbsp chili powder
- Salt and black pepper, to taste
- 6 tbsp cajun seasoning
- 3 tbsp olive oil

Directions:

1. In a pot over medium heat warm olive oil. Add the sausages, chicken, pepper, onion, dry mustard, chili, tomatoes, thyme, bell peppers, salt, oregano, garlic powder, cayenne, and cajun seasoning.
2. Cook for 10 minutes. Add the remaining ingredients and bring to a boil. Reduce the heat and simmer for 20 minutes covered. Serve hot divided between bowls.

Nutrition Info:

- Info Per Servings 6g Carbs, 26g Protein, 22g Fat, 361 Calories

Roasted Chicken With Tarragon

Servings: 4
Cooking Time: 50 Minutes
Ingredients:

- 2 lb chicken thighs
- 2 lb radishes, sliced
- 4 ¼ oz butter
- 1 tbsp tarragon
- Salt and black pepper, to taste
- 1 cup mayonnaise

Directions:

1. Set an oven to 400ºF and grease a baking dish. Add in the chicken, radishes, tarragon, pepper, and salt. Place in butter then set into the oven and cook for 40 minutes. Kill the heat, set on a serving plate and enjoy alongside mayonnaise.

Nutrition Info:

- Info Per Servings 5.5g Carbs, 42g Protein, 23g Fat, 415 Calories

Bacon And Chicken Cottage Pie

Servings: 4

Cooking Time: 55 Minutes

Ingredients:

- ½ cup onion, chopped
- 4 bacon slices
- 3 tbsp butter
- 1 carrot, chopped
- 3 garlic cloves, minced
- Salt and ground black pepper, to taste
- ¾ cup crème fraîche
- ½ cup chicken stock
- 12 ounces chicken breasts, cubed
- 2 tbsp Dijon mustard
- ¾ cup cheddar cheese, shredded
- For the dough
- ¾ cup almond flour
- 3 tbsp cream cheese
- 1½ cup mozzarella cheese, shredded
- 1 egg
- 1 tsp onion powder
- 1 tsp garlic powder
- 1 tsp Italian seasoning
- Salt and ground black pepper, to taste

Directions:

1. Set a pan over medium heat and warm butter and sauté the onion, garlic, pepper, bacon, salt, and carrot, for 5 minutes. Add in the chicken, and cook for 3 minutes. Stir in the crème fraîche, salt, mustard, pepper, and stock, cook for 7 minutes. Add in the cheddar and set aside.

2. Using a bowl, combine the mozzarella cheese with the cream cheese, and heat in a microwave for 1 minute. Stir in the garlic powder, salt, flour, pepper, Italian seasoning, onion powder, and egg. Knead the dough well, split into 4 pieces, and flatten each into a circle. Set the chicken mixture into 4 ramekins, top each with a dough circle, place in an oven at 370° F for 25 minutes.

Nutrition Info:

- Info Per Servings 8.2g Carbs, 41g Protein, 45g Fat, 571 Calories

Turkey Enchilada Bowl

Servings: 4

Cooking Time: 30 Minutes

Ingredients:

- 2 tbsp coconut oil
- 1 lb boneless, skinless turkey thighs, cut into pieces
- ¾ cup red enchilada sauce (sugar-free)
- ¼ cup water
- ¼ cup chopped onion
- 3 oz canned diced green chilis
- 1 avocado, diced
- 1 cup shredded mozzarella cheese
- ¼ cup chopped pickled jalapeños
- ½ cup sour cream
- 1 tomato, diced

Directions:

1. Set a large pan over medium-high heat. Add coconut oil and warm. Place in the turkey and cook until browned on the outside. Stir in onion, chillis, water, and enchilada sauce, then close with a lid.

2. Allow simmering for 20 minutes until the turkey is cooked through. Spoon the turkey on a serving bowl and top with the sauce, cheese, sour cream, tomato, and avocado.

Nutrition Info:

- Info Per Servings 5.9g Carbs, 38g Protein, 40.2g Fat, 568 Calories

Chicken And Spinach

Servings: 8
Cooking Time: 50 Minutes
Ingredients:

- 1-pound chicken breasts
- 2 jars commercial pasta sauce
- 2 cups baby spinach
- 1 onion chopped
- ¼ cup cheese
- 5 tbsps oil
- ½ cup water
- Pepper and salt to taste

Directions:

1. Place a heavy-bottomed pot on medium-high fire and heat pot for 2 minutes.
2. Add oil and swirl to coat sides and bottom of the pot. Heat oil for a minute.
3. Season chicken breasts with pepper and salt. Brown chicken for 4 minutes per side. Transfer to a chopping board and cut into ½-inch cubes.
4. In the same pot, sauté onions for 5 minutes. Add pasta sauce and season with pepper and salt. Stir in water and chicken breasts. Simmer pasta sauce for 30 minutes on low fire. Stir the bottom of the pot every now and then.
5. Mix spinach in a pot of sauce. Let it rest for 5 minutes.
6. Serve and enjoy with a sprinkle of cheese.

Nutrition Info:

- Info Per Servings 6.7g Carbs, 21.2g Protein, 15.6g Fat, 216 Calories

Simple Chicken Garlic-tomato Stew

Servings: 4
Cooking Time: 45 Minutes
Ingredients:

- 3 tbsp. coconut oil
- 5 cloves of garlic, minced
- 4 chicken breasts halves
- 3 roma tomatoes chopped
- 1 small onion chopped
- Salt and pepper to taste
- 1 ½ cups water

Directions:

1. Place a large saucepan on medium-high fire and heat for 2 minutes.
2. Add 1 tbsp oil and heat for a minute.
3. Season chicken breasts generously with pepper and salt.
4. Sear for 5 minutes per side of the chicken breast. Transfer to a plate and let it rest.
5. In the same pan, add remaining oil and sauté garlic for a minute. Stir in onions and tomatoes. Sauté for 7 minutes.
6. Meanwhile, chop chicken into bite-sized pieces.
7. Deglaze pan with water and add chopped chicken. Cover and simmer for 15 minutes.
8. Adjust seasoning if needed.
9. Serve and enjoy.

Nutrition Info:

- Info Per Servings 1.1g Carbs, 60.8g Protein, 37.5g Fat, 591 Calories

Pancetta & Chicken Casserole

Servings: 3
Cooking Time: 40 Minutes
Ingredients:
- 8 pancetta strips, chopped
- ⅓ cup Dijon mustard
- Salt and black pepper, to taste
- 1 onion, chopped
- 1 tbsp olive oil
- 1½ cups chicken stock
- 3 chicken breasts, skinless and boneless
- ¼ tsp sweet paprika

Directions:

1. Using a bowl, combine the paprika, pepper, salt, and mustard. Sprinkle this on chicken breasts and massage. Set a pan over medium-high heat, stir in the pancetta, cook until it browns, and remove to a plate. Place oil in the same pan and heat over medium-high heat, add in the chicken breasts, cook for each side for 2 minutes and set aside.

2. Place in the stock, and bring to a simmer. Stir in pepper, pancetta, salt, and onion. Return the chicken to the pan as well, stir gently, and simmer for 20 minutes over medium heat, turning the meat halfway through. Split the chicken on serving plates, sprinkle the sauce over it to serve.

Nutrition Info:
- Info Per Servings 3g Carbs, 26g Protein, 18g Fat, 313 Calories

Cheese Stuffed Chicken Breasts With Spinach

Servings: 4
Cooking Time: 50 Minutes
Ingredients:
- 4 chicken breasts, boneless and skinless
- ½ cup mozzarella cheese
- ⅓ cup Parmesan cheese
- 6 ounces cream cheese
- 2 cups spinach, chopped
- A pinch of nutmeg
- ½ tsp minced garlic
- Breading:
- 2 eggs
- ⅓ cup almond flour
- 2 tbsp olive oil
- ½ tsp parsley
- ⅓ cup Parmesan cheese
- A pinch of onion powder

Directions:

1. Pound the chicken until it doubles in size. Mix the cream cheese, spinach, mozzarella, nutmeg, salt, pepper, and parmesan in a bowl. Divide the mixture between the chicken breasts and spread it out evenly. Wrap the chicken in a plastic wrap. Refrigerate for 15 minutes.

2. Heat the oil in a pan and preheat the oven to 370ºF. Beat the eggs and combine all other breading ingredients in a bowl. Dip the chicken in egg first, then in the breading mixture. Cook in the pan until browned. Place on a lined baking sheet and bake for 20 minutes.

Nutrition Info:
- Info Per Servings 3.5g Carbs, 38g Protein, 36g Fat, 491 Calories

Pork, Beef & Lamb Recipes

Peanut Butter Pork Stir-fry

Servings: 4

Cooking Time: 23 Minutes

Ingredients:

- 1 ½ tbsp ghee
- 2 lb pork loin, cut into strips
- Pink salt and chili pepper to taste
- 2 tsp ginger- garlic paste
- ¼ cup chicken broth
- 5 tbsp peanut butter
- 2 cups mixed stir-fry vegetables

Directions:

1. Melt the ghee in a wok and mix the pork with salt, chili pepper, and ginger-garlic paste. Pour the pork into the wok and cook for 6 minutes until no longer pink.
2. Mix the peanut butter with some broth to be smooth, add to the pork and stir; cook for 2 minutes. Pour in the remaining broth, cook for 4 minutes, and add the mixed veggies. Simmer for 5 minutes.
3. Adjust the taste with salt and black pepper, and spoon the stir-fry to a side of cilantro cauli rice.

Nutrition Info:

- Info Per Servings 1g Carbs, 22.5g Protein, 49g Fat, 571 Calories

Beef Brisket In Mustard Sauce

Servings: 7

Cooking Time: 60 Minutes

Ingredients:

- 2 ½ pounds beef brisket, cut into 2-inch cubes
- ½ cup onion, chopped
- 1 tablespoon prepared mustard
- ½ cup olive oil
- Salt and pepper to taste
- 1 cup water

Directions:

1. Place all ingredients in a heavy-bottomed pot on high fire and bring to a boil.
2. Once boiling, lower fire to a simmer.
3. Simmer for 60 minutes.
4. Serve and enjoy.

Nutrition Info:

- Info Per Servings 1.7g Carbs, 29.4g Protein, 39.2g Fat, 477 Calories

Mustardy Pork Chops

Servings: 4

Cooking Time: 15 Minutes

Ingredients:

- 4 pork loin chops
- 1 tsp Dijon mustard
- 1 tbsp soy sauce
- 1 tsp lemon juice
- 1 tbsp water
- Salt and black pepper, to taste
- 1 tbsp butter
- A bunch of scallions, chopped

Directions:

1. Using a bowl, combine the water with lemon juice, mustard and soy sauce. Set a pan over medium heat and warm butter, add in the pork chops, season with salt, and pepper, cook for 4 minutes, turn, and cook for additional 4 minutes. Remove the pork chops to a plate and keep warm.

2. In the same pan, pour in the mustard sauce, and simmer for 5 minutes. Spread this over pork, top with scallions, and enjoy.

Nutrition Info:

- Info Per Servings 1.2g Carbs, 38g Protein, 21.5g Fat, 382 Calories

Beef Stovies

Servings: 4

Cooking Time: 60 Minutes

Ingredients:

- 1 lb ground beef
- 1 large onion, chopped
- 6 parsnips, peeled and chopped
- 1 large carrot, chopped
- 1 tbsp olive oil
- 1 clove garlic, minced
- Salt and black pepper to taste
- 1 cup chicken broth
- ¼ tsp allspice
- 2 tsp rosemary leaves
- 1 tbsp sugar-free Worcestershire sauce
- ½ small cabbage, shredded

Directions:

1. Heat the oil in a skillet over medium heat and cook the beef for 4 minutes. Season with salt and pepper, and occasionally stir while breaking the lumps in it.

2. Add the onion, garlic, carrots, rosemary, and parsnips. Stir and cook for a minute, and pour the chicken broth, allspice, and Worcestershire sauce in it. Stir the mixture and cook the ingredients on low heat for 40 minutes.

3. Stir in the cabbage, season with salt and pepper, and cook the ingredients further for 2 minutes. After, turn the heat off, plate the stovies, and serve with wilted spinach and collards.

Nutrition Info:

- Info Per Servings 3g Carbs, 14g Protein, 18g Fat, 316 Calories

Simple Beef Curry

Servings: 6
Cooking Time:30 Minutes
Ingredients:
- 2 pounds boneless beef chuck
- 1 tbsp ground turmeric
- 1 tsp ginger paste
- 6 cloves garlic, minced
- 1 onion, chopped
- 3 tbsp olive oil
- 1 cup water
- Pepper and salt to taste

Directions:
1. In a saucepan, heat the olive oil over medium heat then add onion and garlic for 5 minutes.
2. Stir in beef and sauté for 10 minutes.
3. Add remaining ingredients, cover, and simmer for 20 minutes.
4. Adjust seasoning if needed.
5. Serve and enjoy.

Nutrition Info:
- Info Per Servings 5.0g Carbs, 33.0g Protein, 16.0g Fat, 287 Calories

Beef Italian Sandwiches

Servings: 6
Cooking Time: 40 Minutes
Ingredients:
- 6 Provolone cheese slices
- 14.5-ounce can beef broth
- 8-ounces giardiniera drained (Chicago-style Italian sandwich mix)
- 3-pounds chuck roast fat trimmed and cut into large pieces
- 6 large lettuce
- Pepper and salt to taste

Directions:
1. Add all ingredients in a pot, except for lettuce and cheese, on high fire, and bring to a boil.
2. Once boiling, lower fire to a simmer and cook for 25 minutes.
3. Adjust seasoning to taste.
4. To make a sandwich, add warm shredded beef in one lettuce leaf and top with cheese.

Nutrition Info:
- Info Per Servings 3.9g Carbs, 48.6g Protein, 36.4g Fat, 538 Calories

Lemon Pork Chops With Buttered Brussels Sprouts

Servings: 6
Cooking Time: 27 Minutes

Ingredients:

- 3 tbsp lemon juice
- 3 cloves garlic, pureed
- 1 tbsp olive oil
- 6 pork loin chops
- 1 tbsp butter
- 1 lb brussels sprouts, trimmed and halved
- 2 tbsp white wine
- Salt and black pepper to taste

Directions:

1. Preheat broiler to 400ºF and mix the lemon juice, garlic, salt, pepper, and oil in a bowl.
2. Brush the pork with the mixture, place in a baking sheet, and cook for 6 minutes on each side until browned. Share into 6 plates and make the side dish.
3. Melt butter in a small wok or pan and cook in brussels sprouts for 5 minutes until tender. Drizzle with white wine, sprinkle with salt and black pepper and cook for another 5 minutes.
4. Ladle brussels sprouts to the side of the chops and serve with a hot sauce.

Nutrition Info:

- Info Per Servings 2g Carbs, 26g Protein, 48g Fat, 549 Calories

Simple Corned Beef

Servings: 6
Cooking Time: 1 Hour And 30 Minutes

Ingredients:

- 2 pounds corned beef brisket, cut into 1-inch cubes
- 2 cups water
- 2 onions, chopped
- 6 garlic cloves, smashed
- 1 cup olive oil
- 1 tbsp peppercorns
- 1 tsp salt

Directions:

1. Place all ingredients in a heavy-bottomed pot on high fire and bring to a boil.
2. Once boiling, lower fire to a simmer.
3. Simmer for 60 minutes.
4. Turn off fire and shred beef with two forks.
5. Turn on fire and continue cooking until sauce is reduced.
6. Serve and enjoy.

Nutrition Info:

- Info Per Servings 0.6g Carbs, 12.1g Protein, 30.2g Fat, 314 Calories

White Wine Lamb Chops

Servings: 6

Cooking Time: 1 Hour And 25 Minutes

Ingredients:

- 6 lamb chops
- 1 tbsp sage
- 1 tsp thyme
- 1 onion, sliced
- 3 garlic cloves, minced
- 2 tbsp olive oil
- ½ cup white wine
- Salt and black pepper, to taste

Directions:

1. Heat the olive oil in a pan. Add onion and garlic and cook for 3 minutes, until soft. Rub the sage and thyme over the lamb chops. Cook the lamb for about 3 minutes per side. Set aside.

2. Pour the white wine and 1 cup of water into the pan, bring the mixture to a boil. Cook until the liquid is reduced by half. Add the chops in the pan, reduce the heat, and let simmer for 1 hour.

Nutrition Info:

- Info Per Servings 4.3g Carbs, 16g Protein, 30g Fat, 397 Calories

Pork Lettuce Cups

Servings: 6

Cooking Time: 20 Minutes

Ingredients:

- 2 lb ground pork
- 1 tbsp ginger- garlic paste
- Pink salt and chili pepper to taste
- 1 tsp ghee
- 1 head Iceberg lettuce
- 2 sprigs green onion, chopped
- 1 red bell pepper, seeded and chopped
- ½ cucumber, finely chopped

Directions:

1. Put the pork with ginger-garlic paste, salt, and chili pepper seasoning in a saucepan. Cook for 10 minutes over medium heat while breaking any lumps until the pork is no longer pink. Drain liquid and add the ghee, melt and brown the meat for 4 minutes, continuously stirring. Turn the heat off.

2. Pat the lettuce dry with paper towel and in each leaf, spoon two to three tablespoons of pork, top with green onions, bell pepper, and cucumber. Serve with soy drizzling sauce.

Nutrition Info:

- Info Per Servings 1g Carbs, 19g Protein, 24.3g Fat, 311 Calories

Ground Beef And Cabbage Stir Fry

Servings: 5

Cooking Time:20 Minutes

Ingredients:

- 1 onion, chopped
- 3 cloves of garlic, minced
- 1 ½ pounds ground beef
- 1 tablespoon grated ginger
- ½ head cabbage, chopped
- 2 tablespoons oil
- Salt and pepper to taste
- 1 teaspoon chili flakes (optional)

Directions:

1. In a skillet, heat oil over medium flame.
2. Sauté the onion and garlic until fragrant.
3. Stir in the ground beef and season with salt and pepper to taste. Cook and crumble for 10 minutes.
4. Add grated ginger, chopped cabbage, and chili flakes. Cover and cook for 5 minutes.
5. Stir and continue cooking for another 3 minutes or until cabbage is translucent and wilted.
6. Serve and enjoy.

Nutrition Info:

- Info Per Servings 6.3g Carbs, 30.6g Protein, 23.7g Fat, 385 Calories

Pancetta Sausage With Kale

Servings: 10
Cooking Time: 25 Minutes
Ingredients:

- ½ gallon chicken broth
- A drizzle of olive oil
- 1 cup heavy cream
- 2 cups kale
- 6 pancetta slices, chopped
- 1 pound radishes, chopped
- 2 garlic cloves, minced
- Salt and black pepper, to taste
- A pinch of red pepper flakes
- 1 onion, chopped
- 1½ pounds hot pork sausage, chopped

Directions:

1. Set a pot over medium heat. Add in a drizzle of olive oil and warm. Stir in garlic, onion, pancetta, and sausage; cook for 5 minutes. Pour in broth, radishes, and kale, and simmer for 10 minutes.
2. Stir in the, salt, red pepper flakes, pepper, and heavy cream, and cook for about 5 minutes. Split among serving bowls and enjoy the meal.

Nutrition Info:

- Info Per Servings 5.4g Carbs, 21g Protein, 29g Fat, 386 Calories

Roasted Spicy Beef

Servings: 4
Cooking Time: 70 Minutes
Ingredients:

- 2 lb beef brisket
- Salt and black pepper, to taste
- ½ tsp celery salt
- 1 tsp chili powder
- 1 tbsp avocado oil
- 1 tbsp sweet paprika
- A pinch of cayenne pepper
- ½ tsp garlic powder
- ½ cup beef stock
- 1 tbsp garlic, minced
- ¼ tsp dry mustard

Directions:

1. Preheat your oven to 340ºF. In a bowl, combine the paprika with dry mustard, chili powder, salt, garlic powder, cayenne pepper, and celery salt. Rub the meat with this mixture.
2. Set a pan over medium-high heat and warm avocado oil, place in the beef, and sear until brown. Remove to a baking dish. Pour in the stock, add garlic and bake for 60 minutes.
3. Set the beef to a cutting board, leave to cool before slicing and splitting in serving plates. Take the juices from the baking dish and strain, sprinkle over the meat, and enjoy.

Nutrition Info:

- Info Per Servings 3.5g Carbs, 55g Protein, 23.5g Fat, 480 Calories

Grilled Pork Loin Chops With Barbecue Sauce

Servings: 4

Cooking Time: 1 Hour 50 Minutes

Ingredients:

- 4 thick-cut pork loin chops, boneless
- ½ cup sugar-free BBQ sauce
- 1 tsp black pepper
- 1 tbsp erythritol
- ½ tsp ginger powder
- 2 tsp sweet paprika

Directions:

1. In a bowl, mix the black pepper, erythritol, ginger powder, and sweet paprika, and rub the pork chops on all sides with the mixture. Then, cover the pork chops with plastic wraps and place it in the refrigerator to marinate for 1 hour 30 minutes.
2. Preheat the grill to 450ºF. Unwrap the meat, place on the grill grate, and cook for 2 minutes per side. Reduce the heat and brush the BBQ sauce on the meat, cover and grill them for 5 minutes.
3. Open the lid, turn the meat and brush again with barbecue sauce. Continue cooking covered for 5 minutes. Remove the meat to a serving platter and serve with mixed steamed vegetables.

Nutrition Info:

- Info Per Servings 0g Carbs, 34.1g Protein, 26.6g Fat, 363 Calories

Parsley Beef Burgers

Servings: 6

Cooking Time: 25 Minutes

Ingredients:

- 2 pounds ground beef
- 1 tbsp onion flakes
- ¾ almond flour
- ¼ cup beef broth
- 1 tbsp chopped parsley
- 1 tbsp Worcestershire sauce

Directions:

1. Combine all ingredients in a bowl. Mix well with your hands and make 6 patties out of the mixture. Arrange on a lined baking sheet. Bake at 370ºF, for about 18 minutes, until nice and crispy.

Nutrition Info:

- Info Per Servings 2.5g Carbs, 27g Protein, 28g Fat, 354 Calories

Zoodle, Bacon, Spinach, And Halloumi Gratin

Servings: 4
Cooking Time: 35 Minutes
Ingredients:

- 2 large zucchinis, spiralized
- 4 slices bacon, chopped
- 2 cups baby spinach
- 4 oz halloumi cheese, cut into cubes
- 2 cloves garlic, minced
- 1 cup heavy cream
- ½ cup sugar-free tomato sauce
- 1/6 cup water
- 1 cup grated mozzarella cheese
- ½ tsp dried Italian mixed herbs
- Salt and black pepper to taste

Directions:

1. Preheat the oven to 350ºF. Place the cast iron pan over medium heat and fry the bacon for 4 minutes, then add garlic and cook for 1 minute.
2. In a bowl, mix the heavy cream, tomato sauce, and water, and add it to the pan. Stir in the zucchini, spinach, halloumi, Italian herbs, salt, and pepper to taste.
3. Turn the heat off, sprinkle the mozzarella cheese on top, and transfer the pan to the oven. Bake for 20 minutes or until the cheese is golden.
4. When ready, remove the pan and serve the gratin warm with a low carb baguette.

Nutrition Info:

- Info Per Servings 5.3g Carbs, 16g Protein, 27g Fat, 350 Calories

Beef And Ale Pot Roast

Servings: 6
Cooking Time: 2 Hours 20 Minutes
Ingredients:

- 1 ½ lb brisket
- 1 tbsp olive oil
- 8 baby carrots, peeled
- 2 medium red onions, quartered
- 4 stalks celery, cut into chunks
- Salt and black pepper to taste
- 2 bay leaves
- 1 ½ cups low carb beer (ale)

Directions:

1. Preheat the oven to 370ºF. Heat the olive oil in a large skillet, while heating, season the brisket with salt and pepper. Brown the meat on both sides for 8 minutes. After, transfer to a deep casserole dish.
2. In the dish, arrange the carrots, onions, celery, and bay leaves around the brisket and pour the beer all over it. Cover the pot and cook the ingredients in the oven for 2 hours.
3. When ready, remove the casserole. Transfer the beef to a chopping board and cut it into thick slices. Serve the beef and vegetables with a drizzle of the sauce and with steamed turnips.

Nutrition Info:

- Info Per Servings 6g Carbs, 26g Protein, 34g Fat, 513 Calories

Pulled Pork With Avocado

Servings: 12
Cooking Time: 2 Hours 55 Minutes
Ingredients:

- 4 pounds pork shoulder
- 1 tbsp avocado oil
- ½ cup beef stock
- ¼ cup jerk seasoning
- 6 avocado, sliced

Directions:

1. Rub the pork shoulder with jerk seasoning, and set in a greased baking dish. Pour in the stock, and cook for 1 hour 45 minutes in your oven at 350ºF covered with aluminium foil.
2. Discard the foil and cook for another 20 minutes. Leave to rest for 30 minutes, and shred it with 2 forks. Serve topped with avocado slices.

Nutrition Info:

- Info Per Servings 4.1g Carbs, 42g Protein, 42.6g Fat, 567 Calories

Mushroom Pork Chops

Servings: 4
Cooking Time: 45 Minutes
Ingredients:

- 4 pork chops
- 3 cloves of garlic, chopped
- 1 onion, chopped
- 1 lb. fresh mushrooms, sliced
- 4 tbsp butter
- What you'll need from the store cupboard:
- Salt and pepper to taste
- 1 tbsp water
- 5 tbsp oil

Directions:

1. In a large saucepan, place on medium fire and heat oil for 3 minutes. Season pork chops with salt and pepper.
2. Cook for 4 minutes per side the porkchop, until lightly browned. Transfer to a plate and let it rest.
3. In the same pan, add butter. Increase fire to medium-high and sauté garlic. Stir in onions, water, and mushrooms. Sauté until mushrooms are tender, around 7 minutes. Season with salt and pepper.
4. Serve pork chops topped with mushroom mixture.

Nutrition Info:

- Info Per Servings 7.7g Carbs, 46.8g Protein, 47.9g Fat, 649 Calories

Slow Cooker Pork

Servings: 10
Cooking Time: 10 Hours
Ingredients:

- 3 lb. boneless pork loin roast
- ¼ cup Dijon mustard
- 1 tsp. dried thyme leaves
- 2 bay leaves
- 5 tablespoons olive oil
- Salt and pepper to taste
- 1 ½ cups water

Directions:

1. Place all ingredients in the slow cooker.
2. Season with salt and pepper and give a good stir.
3. Cover and cook on low for 10 hours.
4. Serve and enjoy.

Nutrition Info:

- Info Per Servings 0.4g Carbs, 30.7g Protein, 15.7g Fat, 245 Calories

Spiced Pork Roast With Collard Greens

Servings: 4
Cooking Time: 40 Minutes
Ingredients:

- 2 tbsp olive oil
- Salt and black pepper, to taste
- 1 ½ pounds pork loin
- A pinch of dry mustard
- 1 tsp hot red pepper flakes
- ½ tsp ginger, minced
- 1 cup collard greens, chopped
- 2 garlic cloves, minced
- ½ lemon sliced
- ¼ cup water

Directions:

1. Using a bowl, combine the ginger with salt, mustard, and pepper. Add in the meat, toss to coat. Heat the oil in a saucepan over medium-high heat, brown the pork on all sides, for 10 minutes.
2. Transfer to the oven and roast for 1 hour at 390 F. To the saucepan, add collard greens, lemon slices, garlic, and water; cook for 10 minutes. Serve on a platter, sprinkle pan juices on top and enjoy.

Nutrition Info:

- Info Per Servings 3g Carbs, 45g Protein, 23g Fat, 430 Calories

Jamaican Pork Oven Roast

Servings: 12
Cooking Time: 4 Hours And 20 Minutes
Ingredients:

- 4 pounds pork roast
- 1 tbsp olive oil
- ¼ cup jerk spice blend
- ½ cup vegetable stock
- Salt and ground pepper, to taste

Directions:

1. Rub the pork with olive oil and the spice blend. Heat a dutch oven over medium heat and sear the meat well on all sides; add in the stock. Cover the pot, reduce the heat, and let cook for 4 hours.

Nutrition Info:

- Info Per Servings 0g Carbs, 23g Protein, 24g Fat, 282 Calories

Beef Enchilada Stew

Servings: 4
Cooking Time: 40 Minutes
Ingredients:

- 1 cup Mexican cheese, shredded
- 1 can mild green chilies, drained
- 2 teaspoons garlic salt
- 1 10-ounce can La Victoria mild red enchilada sauce
- 2-lbs London broil beef, sliced into 2-inch cubes
- Pepper and salt to taste

Directions:

1. Add all ingredients in a pot on high fire and bring to a boil.
2. Once boiling, lower fire to a simmer and cook for 25 minutes.
3. Adjust seasoning to taste.
4. Serve and enjoy.

Nutrition Info:

- Info Per Servings 10.1g Carbs, 64.2g Protein, 47.4g Fat, 764 Calories

Bacon Stew With Cauliflower

Servings: 6
Cooking Time: 40 Minutes
Ingredients:

- 8 ounces mozzarella cheese, grated
- 2 cups chicken broth
- ½ tsp garlic powder
- ½ tsp onion powder
- Salt and black pepper, to taste
- 4 garlic cloves, minced
- ¼ cup heavy cream
- 3 cups bacon, chopped
- 1 head cauliflower, cut into florets

Directions:

1. In a pot, combine the bacon with broth, cauliflower, salt, heavy cream, pepper, garlic powder, cheese, onion powder, and garlic, and cook for 35 minutes, share into serving plates, and enjoy.

Nutrition Info:

- Info Per Servings 6g Carbs, 33g Protein, 25g Fat, 380 Calories

Pork Chops And Peppers

Servings: 4
Cooking Time: 20 Minutes
Ingredients:

- 4 thick pork chops
- 1 onion, chopped
- 2 cloves of garlic, minced
- 2 red and yellow bell peppers, seeded and julienned
- Salt and pepper to taste
- 5 tablespoons oil

Directions:

1. In a large saucepan, place on medium fire and heat 1 tsp oil for 3 minutes.
2. Add pork chop and cook for 5 minutes per side. Season pork chops with salt and pepper.
3. Transfer pork chops to a plate and let it rest.
4. In the same pan, add remaining oil. Increase fire to medium-high and sauté garlic. Stir in onions and bell peppers. Sauté until tender and crisp around 5 minutes.
5. Serve pork chops topped with bell pepper mixture.

Nutrition Info:

- Info Per Servings 4.3g Carbs, 23.9g Protein, 16.3g Fat, 245 Calories

Beef Steak Filipino Style

Servings: 6
Cooking Time: 25 Minutes
Ingredients:

- 2 tablespoons coconut oil
- 1 onion, sliced
- 4 beef steaks
- 2 tablespoons lemon juice, freshly squeezed
- ¼ cup coconut aminos
- 1 tsp salt
- Pepper to taste

Directions:

1. In a nonstick fry pan, heat oil on medium-high fire.
2. Pan-fry beef steaks and season with coconut aminos.
3. Cook until dark brown, around 7 minutes per side. Transfer to a plate.
4. Sauté onions in the same pan until caramelized, around 8 minutes. Season with lemon juice and return steaks in the pan. Mix well.
5. Serve and enjoy.

Nutrition Info:

- Info Per Servings 0.7g Carbs, 25.3g Protein, 27.1g Fat, 347 Calories

Fish And Seafood Recipes

Steamed Chili-rubbed Tilapia

Servings: 4
Cooking Time: 15 Minutes
Ingredients:

- 1 lb. tilapia fillet, skin removed
- 2 tbsp. chili powder
- 3 cloves garlic, peeled and minced
- 2 tbsp. extra virgin olive oil
- 2 tbsp soy sauce

Directions:

1. Place a trivet in a large saucepan and pour a cup or two of water into the pan. Bring it to a boil.
2. Place tilapia in a heatproof dish that fits inside a saucepan. Drizzle soy sauce and oil on the filet. Season with chili powder and garlic.
3. Seal dish with foil. Place the dish on the trivet inside the saucepan. Cover and steam for 15 minutes.
4. Serve and enjoy.

Nutrition Info:

- Info Per Servings 2g Carbs, 26g Protein, 10g Fat, 211 Calories

Baked Fish With Feta And Tomato

Serves: 2
Cooking Time: 15 Minutes
Ingredients:

- 2 pacific whitening fillets
- 1 scallion, chopped
- 1 Roma tomato, chopped
- 1 tsp fresh oregano
- 1-ounce feta cheese, crumbled
- Seasoning:
- 2 tbsp avocado oil
- 1/3 tsp salt
- 1/4 tsp ground black pepper
- ¼ crushed red pepper

Directions:

1. Turn on the oven, then set it to 400 °F and let it preheat.Take a medium skillet pan, place it over medium heat, add oil and when hot, add scallion and cook for 3 minutes.Add tomatoes, stir in ½ tsp oregano, 1/8 tsp salt, black pepper, red pepper, pour in ¼ cup water and bring it to simmer.Sprinkle remaining salt over fillets, add to the pan, drizzle with remaining oil, and then bake for 10 to 12 minutes until fillets are fork-tender.When done, top fish with remaining oregano and cheese and then serve.

Nutrition Info:

- 8 g Carbs; 26.7 g Protein; 29.5 g Fats; 427.5 Calories

Lemon-rosemary Shrimps

Servings: 4
Cooking Time: 12 Minutes
Ingredients:

- ½ cup lemon juice, freshly squeezed
- 1 ½ lb. shrimps, peeled and deveined
- 2 tbsp fresh rosemary
- ¼ cup coconut aminos
- 2 tbsp butter
- Pepper to taste
- 4 tbsp olive oil

Directions:

1. Place a nonstick saucepan on medium-high fire and heat oil and butter for 2 minutes.
2. Stir in shrimps and coconut aminos. Season with pepper. Sauté for 5 minutes.
3. Add remaining ingredients and cook for another 5 minutes while stirring frequently.
4. Serve and enjoy.

Nutrition Info:

- Info Per Servings 3.7g Carbs, 35.8g Protein, 22.4g Fat, 359 Calories

Lemon Marinated Salmon With Spices

Servings: 2

Cooking Time: 15 Minutes

Ingredients:

- 2 tablespoons. lemon juice
- 1 tablespoon. yellow miso paste
- 2 teaspoons. Dijon mustard
- 1 pinch cayenne pepper and sea salt to taste
- 2 center-cut salmon fillets, boned; skin on
- 1 1/2 tablespoons mayonnaise
- 1 tablespoon ground black pepper

Directions:

1. In a bowl, combine lemon juice with black pepper. Stir in mayonnaise, miso paste, Dijon mustard, and cayenne pepper, mix well. Pour over salmon fillets, reserve about a tablespoon marinade. Cover and marinate the fish in the refrigerator for 30 minutes.

2. Preheat oven to 450 degrees F. Line a baking sheet with parchment paper.

3. Lay fillets on the prepared baking sheet. Rub the reserved lemon-pepper marinade on fillets. Then season with cayenne pepper and sea salt to taste.

4. Bake in the oven for 10 to 15 minutes until cooked through.

Nutrition Info:

- Info Per Servings 7.1g Carbs, 20g Protein, 28.1g Fat, 361 Calories

Blackened Fish Tacos With Slaw

Servings: 4

Cooking Time: 20 Minutes

Ingredients:

- 1 tbsp olive oil
- 1 tsp chili powder
- 2 tilapia fillets
- 1 tsp paprika
- 4 low carb tortillas
- Slaw:
- ½ cup red cabbage, shredded
- 1 tbsp lemon juice
- 1 tsp apple cider vinegar
- 1 tbsp olive oil

Directions:

1. Season the tilapia with chili powder and paprika. Heat the olive oil in a skillet over medium heat.

2. Add tilapia and cook until blackened, about 3 minutes per side. Cut into strips. Divide the tilapia between the tortillas. Combine all slaw ingredients in a bowl. Split the slaw among the tortillas.

Nutrition Info:

- Info Per Servings 3.5g Carbs, 13.8g Protein, 20g Fat, 268 Calories

Baked Salmon With Pistachio Crust

Serves:4

Cooking Time: 35 Minutes

Ingredients:

- 4 salmon fillets
- ¼ cup mayonnaise
- ½ cup ground pistachios
- 1 chopped shallot
- 2 tsp lemon zest
- 1 tbsp olive oil
- A pinch of pepper
- 1 cup heavy cream

Directions:

1. Preheat oven to 375 °F. Brush salmon with mayo and season with salt and pepper. Coat with pistachios. Place in a lined baking dish and bake for 15 minutes. Heat the olive oil in a saucepan and sauté shallot for 3 minutes. Stir in heavy cream and lemon zest. Bring to a boil and cook until thickened. Serve salmon with the sauce.

Nutrition Info:

- Per Serves 6g Carbs; 34g Protein; 47g Fat ; 563 Calories

Golden Pompano In Microwave

Servings: 2

Cooking Time: 11 Minutes

Ingredients:

- ½-lb pompano
- 1 tbsp soy sauce, low sodium
- 1-inch thumb ginger, diced
- 1 lemon, halved
- 1 stalk green onions, chopped
- ¼ cup water
- 1 tsp pepper
- 4 tbsp olive oil

Directions:

1. In a microwavable casserole dish, mix well all ingredients except for pompano, green onions, and lemon.
2. Squeeze half of the lemon in dish and slice into thin circles the other half.
3. Place pompano in the dish and add lemon circles on top of the fish. Drizzle with pepper and olive oil.
4. Cover top of a casserole dish with a microwave-safe plate.
5. Microwave for 5 minutes.
6. Remove from microwave, turn over fish, sprinkle green onions, top with a microwavable plate.
7. Return to microwave and cook for another 3 minutes.
8. Let it rest for 3 minutes more.
9. Serve and enjoy.

Nutrition Info:

- Info Per Servings 6.3g Carbs, 22.2g Protein, 39.5g Fat, 464 Calories

Steamed Cod With Ginger

Servings: 4

Cooking Time: 15 Minutes

Ingredients:

- 4 cod fillets, skin removed
- 3 tbsp. lemon juice, freshly squeezed
- 2 tbsp. coconut aminos
- 2 tbsp. grated ginger
- 6 scallions, chopped
- 5 tbsp coconut oil
- Pepper and salt to taste

Directions:

1. Place a trivet in a large saucepan and pour a cup or two of water into the pan. Bring to a boil.
2. In a small bowl, whisk well lemon juice, coconut aminos, coconut oil, and grated ginger.
3. Place scallions in a heatproof dish that fits inside a saucepan. Season scallions mon with pepper and salt. Drizzle with ginger mixture. Sprinkle scallions on top.
4. Seal dish with foil. Place the dish on the trivet inside the saucepan. Cover and steam for 15 minutes.
5. Serve and enjoy.

Nutrition Info:

- Info Per Servings 10g Carbs, 28.3g Protein, 40g Fat, 514 Calories

Shrimp Spread

Servings: 20

Cooking Time: 0 Minutes

Ingredients:

- 1 package cream cheese, softened
- 1/2 cup sour cream
- 1 cup seafood cocktail sauce
- 12 ounces frozen cooked salad shrimp, thawed
- 1 medium green pepper, chopped
- Pepper

Directions:

1. In a large bowl, beat the cream cheese, and sour cream until smooth.
2. Spread mixture on a round 12-inch serving platter.
3. Top with seafood sauce.
4. Sprinkle with shrimp and green peppers. Cover and refrigerate.
5. Serve with crackers.

Nutrition Info:

- Info Per Servings 4g Carbs, 8g Protein, 10g Fat, 136 Calories

Alaskan Cod With Mustard Cream Sauce

Serves: 4

Cooking Time: 10 Minutes

Ingredients:

- 1 tablespoon coconut oil
- 4 Alaskan cod fillets
- Salt and freshly ground black pepper, to taste
- 6 leaves basil, chiffonade
- Mustard Cream Sauce:
- 1 teaspoon yellow mustard
- 1 teaspoon paprika
- 1/4 teaspoon ground bay leaf
- 3 tablespoons cream cheese
- 1/2 cup Greek-style yogurt
- 1 garlic clove, minced
- 1 teaspoon lemon zest
- 1 tablespoon fresh parsley, minced
- Sea salt and ground black pepper, to taste

Directions:

1. Heat coconut oil in a pan over medium heat. Sear the fish for 2 to 3 minutes per side. Season with salt and ground black pepper.

2. Mix all ingredients for the sauce until everything is well combined. Top the fish fillets with the sauce and serve garnished with fresh basil leaves. Bon appétit!

Nutrition Info:

- Per Serves 2.6g Carbs; 19.8g Protein; 8.2g Fat; 166 Calories;

Enchilada Sauce On Mahi Mahi

Servings: 2

Cooking Time: 15 Minutes

Ingredients:

- 2 Mahi fillets, fresh
- ¼ cup commercial enchilada sauce
- Pepper to taste

Directions:

1. In a heat-proof dish that fits inside saucepan, place fish and top with enchilada sauce.

2. Place a large saucepan on the medium-high fire. Place a trivet inside the saucepan and fill the pan halfway with water. Cover and bring to a boil.

3. Cover dish with foil and place on a trivet.

4. Cover pan and steam for 10 minutes. Let it rest in pan for another 5 minutes.

5. Serve and enjoy topped with pepper.

Nutrition Info:

- Info Per Servings 8.9g Carbs, 19.8g Protein, 15.9g Fat, 257 Calories

Bacon Wrapped Salmon

Serves: 2

Cooking Time: 15 Minutes

Ingredients:

- 2 6-ounces salmon fillets
- 2 streaky bacon slices
- 4 tablespoons pesto

Directions:

1. Preheat the oven to 350 °F and line a medium baking sheet with parchment paper.

2. Wrap each salmon fillet with 1 bacon slice and then, secure with a wooden skewer.

3. Place 2 tablespoons of pesto in the center of each salmon fillet.

4. Arrange the salmon fillets onto prepared baking sheet.

5. Bake for about 15 minutes.

6. Remove the salmon fillets from oven and transfer onto the serving plates.

7. Serve hot.

Nutrition Info:

- Per Serving: 1.9g Carbs; 46.7g Protein; 35.6g Fat; 57 Calories;

Coconut Milk Sauce Over Crabs

Servings: 6

Cooking Time: 20 Minutes

Ingredients:

- 2-pounds crab quartered
- 1 can coconut milk
- 1 thumb-size ginger, sliced
- 1 onion, chopped
- 3 cloves of garlic, minced
- Pepper and salt to taste

Directions:

1. Place a heavy-bottomed pot on medium-high fire and add all ingredients.
2. Cover and bring to a boil, lower fire to a simmer, and simmer for 20 minutes.
3. Serve and enjoy.

Nutrition Info:

- Info Per Servings 6.3g Carbs, 29.3g Protein, 11.3g Fat, 244.1 Calories

Seasoned Salmon With Parmesan

Servings: 4

Cooking Time: 20 Mins

Ingredients:

- 2 lbs. salmon fillet
- 3 minced garlic cloves
- ¼ cup. chopped parsley
- ½ cup. grated parmesan cheese
- Salt and pepper to taste

Directions:

1. Preheat oven to 425 degrees F. Line a baking sheet with parchment paper.
2. Lay salmon fillets on the lined baking sheet, season with salt and pepper to taste.
3. Bake for 10 minutes. Remove from the oven and sprinkle with garlic, parmesan and parsley.
4. Place in the oven to cook for 5 more minutes. Transfer to plates before serving.

Nutrition Info:

- Info Per Servings 0.6g Carbs, 25g Protein, 12g Fat, 210 Calories

Avocado And Salmon

Serves: 2

Cooking Time: 0 Minutes

Ingredients:

- 1 avocado, halved, pitted
- 2 oz flaked salmon, packed in water
- 1 tbsp mayonnaise
- 1 tbsp grated cheddar cheese
- Seasoning:
- 1/8 tsp salt
- 2 tbsp coconut oil

Directions:

1. Prepare the avocado and for this, cut avocado in half and then remove its seed.Drain the salmon, add it in a bowl along with remaining ingredients, stir well and then scoop into the hollow on an avocado half.Serve.

Nutrition Info:

- 3 g Carbs; 19 g Protein; 48 g Fats; 525 Calories

Flounder With Dill And Capers

Servings: 4

Cooking Time: 15 Minutes

Ingredients:

- 4 flounder fillets
- 1 tbsp. chopped fresh dill
- 2 tbsp. capers, chopped
- 4 lemon wedges
- 6 tbsp olive oil
- Salt and pepper to taste

Directions:

1. Place a trivet in a large saucepan and pour a cup or two of water into the pan. Bring to a boil.
2. Place flounder in a heatproof dish that fits inside a saucepan. Season snapper with pepper and salt. Drizzle with olive oil on all sides. Sprinkle dill and capers on top of the filet.
3. Seal dish with foil. Place the dish on the trivet inside the saucepan. Cover and steam for 15 minutes.
4. Serve and enjoy with lemon wedges.

Nutrition Info:

- Info Per Servings 8.6g Carbs, 20.3g Protein, 35.9g Fat, 447 Calories

Shrimp In Curry Sauce

Servings: 2

Cooking Time: 25 Minutes

Ingredients:

- ½ ounces grated Parmesan cheese
- 1 tbsp water
- 1 egg, beaten
- ¼ tsp curry powder
- 2 tsp almond flour
- 12 shrimp, shelled
- 3 tbsp coconut oil
- Sauce
- 2 tbsp curry leaves
- 2 tbsp butter
- ½ onion, diced
- ½ cup heavy cream
- ½ ounce cheddar

Directions:

1. Combine all dry ingredients for the batter. Melt the coconut oil in a skillet over medium heat. Dip the shrimp in the egg first, and then coat with the dry mixture. Fry until golden and crispy.
2. In another skillet, melt the butter. Add onion and cook for 3 minutes. Add curry leaves and cook for 30 seconds. Stir in heavy cream and cheddar and cook until thickened. Add the shrimp and coat well. Serve warm.

Nutrition Info:

- Info Per Servings 4.3g Carbs, 24.4g Protein, 41g Fat, 560 Calories

Salmon Panzanella

Servings: 4

Cooking Time: 22 Minutes

Ingredients:

- 1 lb skinned salmon, cut into 4 steaks each
- 1 cucumber, peeled, seeded, cubed
- Salt and black pepper to taste
- 8 black olives, pitted and chopped
- 1 tbsp capers, rinsed
- 2 large tomatoes, diced
- 3 tbsp red wine vinegar
- ¼ cup thinly sliced red onion
- 3 tbsp olive oil
- 2 slices day-old zero carb bread, cubed
- ¼ cup thinly sliced basil leaves

Directions:

1. Preheat a grill to 350ºF and prepare the salad. In a bowl, mix the cucumbers, olives, pepper, capers, tomatoes, wine vinegar, onion, olive oil, bread, and basil leaves. Let sit for the flavors to incorporate.

2. Season the salmon steaks with salt and pepper; grill them on both sides for 8 minutes in total. Serve the salmon steaks warm on a bed of the veggies' salad.

Nutrition Info:

- Info Per Servings 3.1g Carbs, 28.5g Protein, 21.7g Fat, 338 Calories

Cedar Salmon With Green Onion

Servings: 5

Cooking Time: 20 Mins

Ingredients:

- 3 untreated cedar planks
- 1/4 cup. chopped green onions
- 1 tablespoon. grated fresh ginger root
- 1 teaspoon. minced garlic
- 2 salmon fillets, skin removed
- 1/3 cup. olive oil
- 1/3 cup. mayo
- 1 1/2 tablespoons. rice vinegar

Directions:

1. Soak cedar planks in warm water for 1 hour more.

2. Whisk olive oil, rice vinegar, mayo, green onions, ginger, and garlic in a bowl. Marinade salmon fillets to coat completely. Cover the bowl with plastic wrap and marinate for 15 to 60 minutes.

3. Preheat an outdoor grill over medium heat. Lay planks on the center of hot grate Place the salmon fillets onto the planks and remove the marinade. Cover the grill and cook until cooked through, about 20 minutes, or until salmon is done to your liking. Serve the salmon on a platter right off the planks.

Nutrition Info:

- Info Per Servings 10g Carbs, 18g Protein, 27g Fat, 355 Calories

Smoked Mackerel Patties

Servings: 6
Cooking Time: 30 Minutes

Ingredients:

- 1 turnip, peeled and diced
- 1 ½ cup water
- Pink salt and chili pepper to taste
- 3 tbsp olive oil + for rubbing
- 4 smoked mackerel steaks, bones removed, flaked
- 3 eggs, beaten
- 2 tbsp mayonnaise
- 1 tbsp pork rinds, crushed

Directions:

1. Bring the turnip to boil in salted water in a saucepan over medium heat for 8 minutes or until tender. Drain the turnip through a colander, transfer to a mixing bowl, and mash the lumps.
2. Add the mackerel, eggs, mayonnaise, pork rinds, salt, and chili pepper. With gloves on your hands, mix and make 6 compact patties.
3. Heat olive oil in a skillet over medium heat and fry the patties for 3 minutes on each side to be golden brown. Remove onto a wire rack to cool. Serve with sesame lime dipping sauce.

Nutrition Info:

- Info Per Servings 2.2g Carbs, 16g Protein, 27.1g Fat, 324 Calories

Angel Hair Shirataki With Creamy Shrimp

Serves:4
Cooking Time: 25 Minutes

Ingredients:

- 2 (8 oz) packs angel hair shirataki noodles
- 1 tbsp olive oil
- 1 lb shrimp, deveined
- 2 tbsp unsalted butter
- 6 garlic cloves, minced
- ½ cup dry white wine
- 1 ½ cups heavy cream
- ½ cup grated Asiago cheese
- 2 tbsp chopped fresh parsley

Directions:

1. Heat olive oil in a skillet, season the shrimp with salt and pepper, and cook on both sides, 2 minutes; set aside. Melt butter in the skillet and sauté garlic. Stir in wine and cook until reduced by half, scraping the bottom of the pan to deglaze. Stir in heavy cream. Let simmer for 1 minute and stir in Asiago cheese to melt. Return the shrimp to the sauce and sprinkle the parsley on top. Bring 2 cups of water to a boi. Strain shirataki pasta and rinse under hot running water. Allow proper draining and pour the shirataki pasta into the boiling water. Cook for 3 minutes and strain again. Place a dry skillet and stir-fry the pasta until dry, 1-2 minutes. Season with salt and plate. Top with the shrimp sauce and serve.

Nutrition Info:

- Per Serves 6.3g Carbs; 33g Protein ; 32g Fats; 493 Calories

Cod With Balsamic Tomatoes

Servings: 4
Cooking Time: 30 Minutes
Ingredients:

- 4 center-cut bacon strips, chopped
- 4 cod fillets
- 2 cups grape tomatoes, halved
- 2 tablespoons balsamic vinegar
- 4 tablespoons olive oil
- 1/2 teaspoon salt
- 1/4 teaspoon pepper

Directions:

1. In a large skillet, heat olive oil and cook bacon over medium heat until crisp, stirring occasionally.
2. Remove with a slotted spoon; drain on paper towels.
3. Sprinkle fillets with salt and pepper. Add fillets to bacon drippings; cook over medium-high heat until fish just begins to flake easily with a fork, 4-6 minutes on each side. Remove and keep warm.
4. Add tomatoes to skillet; cook and stir until tomatoes are softened, 2-4 minutes. Stir in vinegar; reduce heat to medium-low. Cook until sauce is thickened, 1-2 minutes longer.
5. Serve cod with tomato mixture and bacon.

Nutrition Info:

- Info Per Servings 5g Carbs, 26g Protein, 30.4g Fat, 442 Calories

Thyme-sesame Crusted Halibut

Servings: 2
Cooking Time: 15 Minutes
Ingredients:

- 8 oz. halibut, cut into 2 portions
- 1 tbsp. lemon juice, freshly squeezed
- 1 tsp. dried thyme leaves
- 1 tbsp. sesame seeds, toasted
- Salt and pepper to taste

Directions:

1. Place a trivet in a large saucepan and pour a cup or two of water into the pan. Bring it to a boil.
2. Place halibut in a heatproof dish that fits inside a saucepan. Season with lemon juice, salt, and pepper. Sprinkle with dried thyme leaves and sesame seeds.
3. Seal dish with foil. Place the dish on the trivet inside the saucepan. Cover and steam for 15 minutes.
4. Serve and enjoy.

Nutrition Info:

- Info Per Servings 4.2g Carbs, 17.5g Protein, 17.7g Fat, 246 Calories

Steamed Ginger Scallion Fish

Servings:
Cooking Time: 15 Minutes
Ingredients:

- 3 tablespoons soy sauce, low sodium
- 2 tablespoons rice wine
- 1 teaspoon minced ginger
- 1 teaspoon garlic
- 1-pound firm white fish
- Pepper to taste
- 4 tbsps sesame oil

Directions:

1. In a heat-proof dish that fits inside the saucepan, add all ingredients. Mix well.
2. Place a large saucepan on the medium-high fire. Place a trivet inside the saucepan and fill the pan halfway with water. Cover and bring to a boil.
3. Cover dish with foil and place on a trivet.
4. Cover pan and steam for 10 minutes. Let it rest in pan for another 5 minutes.
5. Serve and enjoy.

Nutrition Info:

- Info Per Servings 5.5g Carbs, 44.9g Protein, 23.1g Fat, 409.5 Calories

Avocado Tuna Boats

Serves: 2

Cooking Time: 10 Minutes

Ingredients:

- 4 oz tuna, packed in water, drained1 green onion sliced
- 1 avocado, halved, pitted
- 3 tbsp mayonnaise
- 1/3 tsp salt
- Seasoning:
- ¼ tsp ground black pepper
- ¼ tsp paprika

Directions:

1. Prepare the filling and for this, take a medium bowl, place tuna in it, add green onion, salt, black pepper, paprika and mayonnaise and then stir until well combined.Cut avocado in half lengthwise, then remove the pit and fill with prepared filling.Serve.

Nutrition Info:

- ; 7 g Carbs; 8 g Protein; 19 g Fats; 244 Calories

Red Curry Halibut

Servings: 4

Cooking Time: 15 Minutes

Ingredients:

- 4 halibut fillets, skin removed
- 1 cup chopped tomatoes
- 3 green curry leaves
- 2 tbsp. chopped cilantro
- 1 tbsp. lime juice, freshly squeezed
- 3 tbsp olive oil
- Pepper and salt to taste

Directions:

1. Place a trivet in a large saucepan and pour a cup or two of water into the pan. Bring to a boil.
2. Place halibut in a heatproof dish that fits inside the saucepan. Season halibut with pepper and salt. Drizzle with olive oil. Sprinkle chopped tomatoes, curry leaves, chopped cilantro, and lime juice.
3. Seal dish with foil. Place the dish on the trivet inside the saucepan. Cover and steam for 15 minutes.
4. Serve and enjoy.

Nutrition Info:

- Info Per Servings 1.8g Carbs, 76.1g Protein, 15.5g Fat, 429 Calories

Vegan, Vegetable & Meatless Recipes

Cauliflower Fritters

Servings: 6
Cooking Time: 15 Minutes
Ingredients:
- 1 large cauliflower head, cut into florets
- 2 eggs, beaten
- ½ teaspoon turmeric
- 1 large onion, peeled and chopped
- ½ teaspoon salt
- ¼ teaspoon black pepper
- 6 tablespoons oil

Directions:
1. Place the cauliflower florets in a pot with water.
2. Bring to a boil and drain once cooked.
3. Place the cauliflower, eggs, onion, turmeric, salt, and pepper into the food processor.
4. Pulse until the mixture becomes coarse.
5. Transfer into a bowl. Using your hands, form six small flattened balls and place in the fridge for at least 1 hour until the mixture hardens.
6. Heat the oil in a skillet and fry the cauliflower patties for 3 minutes on each side.
7. Serve and enjoy.

Nutrition Info:
- Info Per Servings 2.28g Carbs, 3.9g Protein, 15.3g Fat, 157 Calories

Creamy Cucumber Avocado Soup

Servings: 4
Cooking Time: 15 Minutes
Ingredients:
- 4 large cucumbers, seeded, chopped
- 1 large avocado, peeled and pitted
- Salt and black pepper to taste
- 2 cups water
- 1 tbsp cilantro, chopped
- 3 tbsp olive oil
- 2 limes, juiced
- 2 tsp minced garlic
- 2 tomatoes, evenly chopped
- 1 chopped avocado for garnish

Directions:
1. Pour the cucumbers, avocado halves, salt, pepper, olive oil, lime juice, cilantro, water, and garlic in the food processor. Puree the ingredients for 2 minutes or until smooth.
2. Pour the mixture in a bowl and top with avocado and tomatoes. Serve chilled with zero-carb bread.

Nutrition Info:
- Info Per Servings 4.1g Carbs, 3.7g Protein, 7.4g Fat, 170 Calories

Cauliflower & Hazelnut Salad

Servings: 4
Cooking Time: 15 Minutes + Chilling Time
Ingredients:

- 1 head cauliflower, cut into florets
- 1 cup green onions, chopped
- 4 ounces bottled roasted peppers, chopped
- ¼ cup extra-virgin olive oil
- 1 tbsp wine vinegar
- 1 tsp yellow mustard
- Salt and black pepper, to taste
- ½ cup black olives, pitted and chopped
- ½ cup hazelnuts, chopped

Directions:

1. Place the cauliflower florets over low heat and steam for 5 minutes; let cool and set aside. Add roasted peppers and green onions in a salad bowl.
2. Using a mixing dish, combine salt, olive oil, mustard, pepper, and vinegar. Sprinkle the mixture over the veggies. Place in the reserved cauliflower and shake to mix well. Top with hazelnut and black olives and serve.

Nutrition Info:

- Info Per Servings 6.6g Carbs, 4.2g Protein, 18g Fat, 221 Calories

Vegetable Tempeh Kabobs

Servings: 4
Cooking Time: 2 Hours 26 Minutes
Ingredients:

- 10 oz tempeh, cut into chunks
- 1 ½ cups water
- 1 red onion, cut into chunks
- 1 red bell pepper, cut chunks
- 1 yellow bell pepper, cut into chunks
- 2 tbsp olive oil
- 1 cup sugar-free barbecue sauce

Directions:

1. Bring the water to boil in a pot over medium heat and once it has boiled, turn the heat off, and add the tempeh. Cover the pot and let the tempeh steam for 5 minutes to remove its bitterness.
2. Drain the tempeh after. Pour the barbecue sauce in a bowl, add the tempeh to it, and coat with the sauce. Cover the bowl and marinate in the fridge for 2 hours.
3. Preheat a grill to 350ºF, and thread the tempeh, yellow bell pepper, red bell pepper, and onion.
4. Brush the grate of the grill with olive oil, place the skewers on it, and brush with barbecue sauce. Cook the kabobs for 3 minutes on each side while rotating and brushing with more barbecue sauce.
5. Once ready, transfer the kabobs to a plate and serve with lemon cauli couscous and a tomato sauce.

Nutrition Info:

- Info Per Servings 3.6g Carbs, 13.2g Protein, 15g Fat, 228 Calories

Brussels Sprouts With Tofu

Servings: 4
Cooking Time: 20 Minutes
Ingredients:

- 2 tbsp olive oil
- 2 garlic cloves, minced
- ½ cup onion, chopped
- 10 ounces tofu, crumbled
- 2 tbsp water
- 2 tbsp soy sauce
- 1 tbsp tomato puree
- ½ pound Brussels sprouts, quartered
- Sea salt and black pepper, to taste

Directions:

1. Set a saucepan over medium-high heat and warm the oil. Add onion and garlic and cook until tender. Place in the soy sauce, water, and tofu. Cook for 5 minutes until the tofu starts to brown.
2. Add in brussels sprouts; apply pepper and salt for seasoning; reduce heat to low and cook for 13 minutes while stirring frequently. Serve while warm.

Nutrition Info:

- Info Per Servings 12.1g Carbs, 10.5g Protein, 11.7g Fat, 179 Calories

Egg And Tomato Salad

Servings: 2
Cooking Time: 1 Minute
Ingredients:

- 4 hard-boiled eggs, peeled and sliced
- 2 red tomatoes, chopped
- 1 small red onion, chopped
- 2 tablespoons lemon juice, freshly squeezed
- Salt and pepper to taste
- 4 tablespoons olive oil

Directions:

1. Place all ingredients in a mixing bowl.
2. Toss to coat all ingredients.
3. Garnish with parsley if desired.
4. Serve over toasted whole wheat bread.

Nutrition Info:

- Info Per Servings 9.1g Carbs, 14.7g Protein, 15.9g Fat, 189 Calories

Strawberry Mug Cake

Servings: 8
Cooking Time: 3 Mins
Ingredients:

- 2 slices fresh strawberry
- 1 teaspoon chia seeds
- 1 teaspoon poppy seeds
- What you'll need from the store cupboard:
- 1/4 teaspoon baking powder
- 3 leaves fresh mint
- 2 tablespoons cream of coconut

Directions:

1. Add all the ingredients together in a mug, stir until finely combined.
2. Cook in microwave at full power for 3 minutes then allow to cool before you serve.

Nutrition Info:

- Info Per Servings 4.7g Carbs, 2.4g Protein, 12g Fat, 196 Calories

Grilled Cauliflower

Servings: 8
Cooking Time: 20 Minutes
Ingredients:

- 1 large head cauliflower
- 1 teaspoon ground turmeric
- 1/2 teaspoon crushed red pepper flakes
- Lemon juice, additional olive oil, and pomegranate seeds, optional
- 2 tablespoons olive oil
- 2 tablespoons melted butter

Directions:

1. Remove leaves and trim stem from cauliflower. Cut cauliflower into eight wedges. Mix turmeric and pepper flakes. Brush wedges with oil; sprinkle with turmeric mixture.
2. Grill, covered, over medium-high heat or broil 4 minutes from heat until cauliflower is tender, 8-10 minutes on each side. If desired, drizzle with lemon juice and additional oil. Brush with melted butter and serve with pomegranate seeds.

Nutrition Info:

- Info Per Servings 2.3g Carbs, 0.7g Protein, 6.3g Fat, 66 Calories

Tofu Sesame Skewers With Warm Kale Salad

Servings: 4
Cooking Time: 2 Hours 40 Minutes
Ingredients:

- 14 oz Firm tofu
- 4 tsp sesame oil
- 1 lemon, juiced
- 5 tbsp sugar-free soy sauce
- 3 tsp garlic powder
- 4 tbsp coconut flour
- ½ cup sesame seeds
- Warm Kale Salad:

- 4 cups chopped kale
- 2 tsp + 2 tsp olive oil
- 1 white onion, thinly sliced
- 3 cloves garlic, minced
- 1 cup sliced white mushrooms
- 1 tsp chopped rosemary
- Salt and black pepper to season
- 1 tbsp balsamic vinegar

Directions:

1. In a bowl, mix sesame oil, lemon juice, soy sauce, garlic powder, and coconut flour. Wrap the tofu in a paper towel, squeeze out as much liquid from it, and cut it into strips. Stick on the skewers, height wise. Place onto a plate, pour the soy sauce mixture over, and turn in the sauce to be adequately coated. Cover the dish with cling film and marinate in the fridge for 2 hours.
2. Heat the griddle pan over high heat. Pour the sesame seeds in a plate and roll the tofu skewers in the seeds for a generous coat. Grill the tofu in the griddle pan to be golden brown on both sides, about 12 minutes in total.
3. Heat 2 tablespoons of olive oil in a skillet over medium heat and sauté onion to begin browning for 10 minutes with continuous stirring. Add the remaining olive oil and mushrooms. Continue cooking for 10 minutes. Add garlic, rosemary, salt, pepper, and balsamic vinegar. Cook for 1 minute.
4. Put the kale in a salad bowl; when the onion mixture is ready, pour it on the kale and toss well. Serve the tofu skewers with the warm kale salad and a peanut butter dipping sauce.

Nutrition Info:

- Info Per Servings 6.1g Carbs, 5.6g Protein, 12.9g Fat, 263 Calories

Guacamole

Servings: 2

Cooking Time: 0 Minutes

Ingredients:

- 2 medium ripe avocados
- 1 tablespoon lemon juice
- 1/4 cup chopped tomatoes
- 4 tablespoons olive oil
- 1/4 teaspoon salt
- Pepper to taste

Directions:

1. Peel and chop avocados; place them in a small bowl. Sprinkle with lemon juice.
2. Add tomatoes and salt.
3. Season with pepper to taste and mash coarsely with a fork. Refrigerate until serving.

Nutrition Info:

- Info Per Servings 10g Carbs, 6g Protein, 56g Fat, 565 Calories

Bell Pepper Stuffed Avocado

Servings: 8

Cooking Time: 10 Minutes

Ingredients:

- 4 avocados, pitted and halved
- 2 tbsp olive oil
- 3 cups green bell peppers, chopped
- 1 onion, chopped
- 1 tsp garlic puree
- Salt and black pepper, to taste
- 1 tsp deli mustard
- 1 tomato, chopped

Directions:

1. From each half of the avocados, scoop out 2 teaspoons of flesh; set aside.
2. Use a sauté pan to warm oil over medium-high heat. Cook the garlic, onion, and bell peppers until tender. Mix in the reserved avocado. Add in tomato, salt, mustard, and black pepper. Separate the mushroom mixture and mix equally among the avocado halves and serve.

Nutrition Info:

- Info Per Servings 7.4g Carbs, 2.4g Protein, 23.2g Fat, 255 Calories

Grilled Spicy Eggplant

Servings: 2

Cooking Time: 20 Minutes

Ingredients:

- 2 small eggplants, cut into 1/2-inch slices
- 1/4 cup olive oil
- 2 tablespoons lime juice
- 3 teaspoons Cajun seasoning
- Salt and pepper to taste

Directions:

1. Brush eggplant slices with oil. Drizzle with lime juice; sprinkle with Cajun seasoning. Let stand for 5 minutes.
2. Grill eggplant, covered, over medium heat or broil 4 minutes. from heat until tender, 4-5 minutes per side.
3. Season with pepper and salt to taste.
4. Serve and enjoy.

Nutrition Info:

- Info Per Servings 7g Carbs, 5g Protein, 28g Fat, 350 Calories

Garlic Lemon Mushrooms

Servings: 4

Cooking Time: 20 Minutes

Ingredients:

- 1/4 cup lemon juice
- 3 tablespoons minced fresh parsley
- 3 garlic cloves, minced
- 1-pound large fresh mushrooms
- 4 tablespoons olive oil
- Pepper to taste

Directions:

1. For the dressing, whisk together the first 5 ingredients. Toss mushrooms with 2 tablespoons dressing.
2. Grill mushrooms, covered, over medium-high heat until tender, 5-7 minutes per side. Toss with remaining dressing before serving.

Nutrition Info:

- Info Per Servings 6.8g Carbs, 4g Protein, 14g Fat, 160 Calories

Pumpkin Bake

Servings: 6

Cooking Time: 45 Minutes

Ingredients:

- 3 large Pumpkins, peeled and sliced
- 1 cup almond flour
- 1 cup grated mozzarella cheese
- 2 tbsp olive oil
- ½ cup chopped parsley

Directions:

1. Preheat the oven to 350ºF. Arrange the pumpkin slices in a baking dish, drizzle with olive oil, and bake for 35 minutes. Mix the almond flour, cheese, and parsley and when the pumpkin is ready, remove it from the oven, and sprinkle the cheese mixture all over. Place back in the oven and grill the top for 5 minutes.

Nutrition Info:

- Info Per Servings 5.7g Carbs, 2.7g Protein, 4.8g Fat, 125 Calories

Chard Swiss Dip

Servings: 6

Cooking Time: 25 Minutes

Ingredients:

- 2 cups Swiss chard
- 1 cup tofu, pressed, drained, crumbled
- ½ cup almond milk
- 2 tsp nutritional yeast
- 2 garlic cloves, minced
- 2 tbsp olive oil
- Salt and pepper to taste
- ½ tsp paprika
- ½ tsp chopped fresh mint leaves

Directions:

1. Set oven to 400ºF. Spray a nonstick cooking spray on a casserole pan. Boil Swiss chard until wilted. Using a blender, puree the remaining ingredients. Season with salt and pepper. Stir in the Swiss chard to get a homogeneous mixture. Bake for 13 minutes. Serve alongside baked vegetables.

Nutrition Info:

- Info Per Servings 7.9g Carbs, 2.9g Protein, 7.3g Fat, 105 Calories

Grilled Cheese The Keto Way

Servings: 1

Cooking Time: 15 Minutes

Ingredients:

- 2 eggs
- ½ tsp baking powder
- 2 tbsp butter
- 2 tbsp almond flour
- 1 ½ tbsp psyllium husk powder
- 2 ounces cheddar cheese

Directions:

1. Whisk together all ingredients except 1 tbsp. butter and cheddar cheese. Place in a square oven-proof bowl, and microwave for 90 seconds. Flip the bun over and cut in half.

2. Place the cheddar cheese on one half of the bun and top with the other. Melt the remaining butter in a skillet. Add the sandwich and grill until the cheese is melted and the bun is crispy.

Nutrition Info:

- Info Per Servings 6.1g Carbs, 25g Protein, 51g Fat, 623 Calories

Morning Coconut Smoothie

Servings: 4

Cooking Time: 5 Minutes

Ingredients:

- ½ cup water
- 1 ½ cups coconut milk
- 1 cup frozen cherries
- 4 cup fresh blueberries
- ¼ tsp vanilla extract
- 1 tbsp vegan protein powder

Directions:

1. Using a blender, combine all the ingredients and blend well until you attain a uniform and creamy consistency. Divide in glasses and serve!

Nutrition Info:

- Info Per Servings 14.9g Carbs, 2.6g Protein, 21.7g Fat, 247 Calories

Cauliflower Mash

Servings: 4

Cooking Time: 10 Minutes

Ingredients:

- 1 head of cauliflower
- ¼ tsp, garlic powder
- 1 handful of chives, chopped
- What you'll need from the store cupboard:
- ¼ tsp, salt
- ¼ tsp, ground black pepper

Directions:

1. Bring a pot of water to boil.
2. Chop cauliflower into florets. Place in a pot of boiling water and boil for 5 minutes.
3. Drain well.
4. Place florets in a blender. Add remaining ingredients except for chives and pulse to desired consistency.
5. Transfer to a bowl and toss in chives.
6. Serve and enjoy.

Nutrition Info:

- Info Per Servings 3.7g Carbs, 1.3g Protein, 0.2g Fat, 18 Calories

Grated Cauliflower With Seasoned Mayo

Servings: 2
Cooking Time: 15 Mins
Ingredients:
- 1 lb grated cauliflower
- 3 oz. butter
- 4 eggs
- 3 oz. pimientos de padron or poblano peppers
- ½ cup mayonnaise
- 1 tsp olive oil
- Salt and pepper
- 1 tsp garlic powder (optional)

Directions:
1. In a bowl, whisk together the mayonnaise and garlic and set aside.
2. Rinse, trim and grate the cauliflower using a food processor or grater.
3. Melt a generous amount of butter and fry grated cauliflower for about 5 minutes. Season salt and pepper to taste.
4. Fry poblanos with oil until lightly crispy. Then fry eggs as you want and sprinkle salt and pepper over them.
5. Serve with poblanos and cauliflower. Drizzle some mayo mixture on top.

Nutrition Info:
- Info Per Servings 9g Carbs, 17g Protein, 87g Fat, 898 Calories

Cheesy Cauliflower Falafel

Servings: 4
Cooking Time: 15 Minutes
Ingredients:
- 1 head cauliflower, cut into florets
- ⅓ cup silvered ground almonds
- ½ tsp mixed spice
- Salt and chili pepper to taste
- 3 tbsp coconut flour
- 3 fresh eggs
- 4 tbsp ghee

Directions:
1. Blend the cauli florets in a food processor until a grain meal consistency is formed. Pour the puree in a bowl, add the ground almonds, mixed spice, salt, chili pepper, and coconut flour, and mix until evenly combined.
2. Beat the eggs in a bowl until creamy in color and mix with the cauli mixture. Shape ¼ cup each into patties and set aside.
3. Melt ghee in a frying pan over medium heat and fry the patties for 5 minutes on each side to be firm and browned. Remove onto a wire rack to cool, share into serving plates, and top with tahini sauce.

Nutrition Info:
- Info Per Servings 2g Carbs, 8g Protein, 26g Fat, 315 Calories

Cauliflower & Mushrooms Stuffed Peppers

Servings: 4

Cooking Time: 40 Minutes

Ingredients:

- 1 head cauliflower
- 4 bell peppers
- 1 cup mushrooms, sliced
- 1 ½ tbsp oil
- 1 onion, chopped
- 1 cup celery, chopped
- 1 garlic cloves, minced
- 1 tsp chili powder
- 2 tomatoes, pureed
- Sea salt and pepper, to taste

Directions:

1. To prepare cauliflower rice, grate the cauliflower into rice-size. Set in a kitchen towel to attract and remove any excess moisture. Set oven to 360ºF.

2. Lightly oil a casserole dish. Chop off bell pepper tops, do away with the seeds and core. Line a baking pan with a parchment paper and roast the peppers for 18 minutes until the skin starts to brown.

3. Warm the oil over medium heat. Add in garlic, celery, and onion and sauté until soft and translucent.Stir in chili powder, mushrooms, and cauliflower rice. Cook for 6 minutes until the cauliflower rice becomes tender. Split the cauliflower mixture among the bell peppers. Set in the casserole dish.Combine pepper, salt, and tomatoes. Top the peppers with the tomato mixture. Bake for 10 minutes.

Nutrition Info:

- Info Per Servings 8.4g Carbs, 1.6g Protein, 4.8g Fat, 77 Calories

Roasted Asparagus With Spicy Eggplant Dip

Servings: 6

Cooking Time: 35 Minutes

Ingredients:

- 1 ½ pounds asparagus spears, trimmed
- ¼ cup olive oil
- 1 tsp sea salt
- ½ tsp black pepper, to taste
- ½ tsp paprika
- For Eggplant Dip
- ¾ pound eggplants
- 2 tsp olive oil
- ½ cup scallions, chopped
- 2 cloves garlic, minced
- 1 tbsp fresh lemon juice
- ½ tsp chili pepper
- Salt and black pepper, to taste
- ¼ cup fresh cilantro, chopped

Directions:

1. Set the oven to 390ºF. Line a parchment paper to a baking sheet. Add asparagus spears to the baking sheet. Toss with oil, paprika, pepper, and salt. Bake until cooked through for 9 minutes.

2. Set the oven to 425 ºF. Add eggplants on a lined cookie sheet. Place under the broiler for about 20 minutes; let the eggplants to cool. Peel them and discard the stems. Place a frying pan over medium-high heat and warm olive oil. Add in garlic and onion and sauté until tender.

3. Using a food processor, pulse together black pepper, roasted eggplants, salt, lemon juice, scallion mixture, and chili pepper to mix evenly. Add cilantro for garnishing. Serve alongside roasted asparagus spears.

Nutrition Info:

- Info Per Servings 9g Carbs, 3.6g Protein, 12.1g Fat, 149 Calories

Paprika 'n Cajun Seasoned Onion Rings

Servings: 6

Cooking Time: 25 Minutes

Ingredients:

- 1 large white onion
- 2 large eggs, beaten
- ½ teaspoon Cajun seasoning
- ¾ cup almond flour
- 1 ½ teaspoon paprika
- ½ cups coconut oil for frying
- ¼ cup water
- Salt and pepper to taste

Directions:

1. Preheat a pot with oil for 8 minutes.
2. Peel the onion, cut off the top and slice into circles.
3. In a mixing bowl, combine the water and the eggs. Season with pepper and salt.
4. Soak the onion in the egg mixture.
5. In another bowl, combine the almond flour, paprika powder, Cajun seasoning, salt and pepper.
6. Dredge the onion in the almond flour mixture.
7. Place in the pot and cook in batches until golden brown, around 8 minutes per batch.

Nutrition Info:

- Info Per Servings 3.9g Carbs, 2.8g Protein, 24.1g Fat, 262 Calories

Morning Granola

Servings: 8

Cooking Time: 1 Hour

Ingredients:

- 1 tbsp coconut oil
- ⅓ cup almond flakes
- ½ cups almond milk
- 2 tbsp sugar
- 1/8 tsp salt
- 1 tsp lime zest
- 1/8 tsp nutmeg, grated
- ½ tsp ground cinnamon
- ½ cup pecans, chopped
- ½ cup almonds, slivered
- 2 tbsp pepitas
- 3 tbsp sunflower seeds
- ¼ cup flax seed

Directions:

1. Set a deep pan over medium-high heat and warm the coconut oil. Add almond flakes and toast for 1 to 2 minutes. Stir in the remaining ingredients. Set oven to 300ºF. Lay the mixture in an even layer onto a baking sheet lined with a parchment paper. Bake for 1 hour, making sure that you shake gently in intervals of 15 minutes. Serve alongside additional almond milk.

Nutrition Info:

- Info Per Servings 9.2g Carbs, 5.1g Protein, 24.3g Fat, 262 Calories

Zoodles With Avocado & Olives

Servings: 4

Cooking Time: 15 Minutes

Ingredients:

- 4 zucchinis, julienned or spiralized
- ½ cup pesto
- 2 avocados, sliced
- 1 cup kalamata olives, chopped
- ¼ cup chopped basil
- 2 tbsp olive oil
- ¼ cup chopped sun-dried tomatoes

Directions:

1. Heat half of the olive oil in a pan over medium heat. Add zoodles and cook for 4 minutes. Transfer to a plate. Stir in pesto, basil, salt, tomatoes, and olives. Top with avocado slices.

Nutrition Info:

- Info Per Servings 8.4g Carbs, 6.3g Protein, 42g Fat, 449 Calories

Cauliflower Gouda Casserole

Servings: 4

Cooking Time: 21 Minutes

Ingredients:

- 2 heads cauliflower, cut into florets
- ⅓ cup butter, cubed
- 2 tbsp melted butter
- 1 white onion, chopped
- Pink salt and black pepper to taste
- ¼ almond milk
- ½ cup almond flour
- 1 ½ cup grated gouda cheese
- Water for sprinkling

Directions:

1. Preheat oven to 350ºF and put the cauli florets in a large microwave-safe bowl. Sprinkle with water, and steam in the microwave for 4 to 5 minutes.

2. Melt the ⅓ cup of butter in a saucepan over medium heat and sauté the onion for 3 minutes. Add the cauliflower, season with salt and black pepper and mix in almond milk. Simmer for 3 minutes.

3. Mix the remaining melted butter with almond flour. Stir into the cauliflower as well as half of the cheese. Sprinkle the top with the remaining cheese and bake for 10 minutes until the cheese has melted and golden brown on the top. Plate the bake and serve with arugula salad.

Nutrition Info:

- Info Per Servings 4g Carbs, 12g Protein, 15g Fat, 215 Calories

Soups, Stew & Salads Recipes

Citrusy Brussels Sprouts Salad

Servings: 6
Cooking Time: 3 Minutes
Ingredients:

- 2 tablespoons olive oil
- ¾ pound Brussels sprouts
- 1 cup walnuts
- Juice from 1 lemon
- ½ cup grated parmesan cheese
- Salt and pepper to taste

Directions:

1. Heat oil in a skillet over medium flame and sauté the Brussels sprouts for 3 minutes until slightly wilted. Removed from heat and allow to cool.
2. In a bowl, toss together the cooled Brussels sprouts and the rest of the ingredients.
3. Toss to coat.

Nutrition Info:

- Info Per Servings 8g Carbs, 6g Protein, 23g Fat, 259 Calories

Chicken Cabbage Soup

Servings: 6
Cooking Time: 30 Minutes
Ingredients:

- 1 can Italian-style tomatoes
- 3 cups chicken broth
- 1 chicken breast
- ½ head of cabbage, shredded
- 1 packet Italian seasoning mix
- Salt and pepper to taste
- 1 cup water
- 1 tsp oil

Directions:

1. Place a heavy-bottomed pot on medium fire and heat for a minute. Add oil and swirl to coat the bottom and sides of the pot.
2. Pan fry chicken breast for 4 minutes per side. Transfer to a chopping board and cut into ½-inch cubes.
3. Add all ingredients to the pot and stir well.
4. Cover and bring to a boil, lower fire to a simmer, and cook for 20 minutes.
5. Adjust seasoning to taste, serve, and enjoy.

Nutrition Info:

- Info Per Servings 5.6g Carbs, 34.1g Protein, 9.3g Fat, 248 Calories

Broccoli Slaw Salad With Mustard-mayo Dressing

Servings: 6
Cooking Time: 10 Minutes
Ingredients:

- 2 tbsp granulated swerve
- 1 tbsp Dijon mustard
- 1 tbsp olive oil
- 4 cups broccoli slaw
- ⅓ cup mayonnaise, sugar-free
- 1 tsp celery seeds
- 1 ½ tbsp apple cider vinegar
- Salt and black pepper, to taste

Directions:

1. Whisk together all ingredients except the broccoli slaw. Place broccoli slaw in a large salad bowl. Pour the dressing over. Mix with your hands to combine well.

Nutrition Info:

- Info Per Servings 2g Carbs, 3g Protein, 10g Fat, 110 Calories

Mexican Soup

Servings: 4

Cooking Time: 25 Minutes

Ingredients:

- 1-pound boneless skinless chicken thighs, cut into 3/4-inch pieces
- 1 tablespoon reduced-sodium taco seasoning
- 1 cup salsa
- 1 carton reduced-sodium chicken broth
- 4 tablespoons olive oil

Directions:

1. In a large saucepan, heat oil over medium-high heat. Add chicken; cook and stir 6-8 minutes or until no longer pink. Stir in taco seasoning.

2. Add remaining ingredients; bring to a boil. Reduce heat; simmer, uncovered, 5 minutes to allow flavors to blend. Skim fat before serving.

Nutrition Info:

- Info Per Servings 5.6g Carbs, 25g Protein, 16.5g Fat, 281 Calories

Cobb Egg Salad In Lettuce Cups

Servings: 4

Cooking Time: 20 Minutes

Ingredients:

- 2 chicken breasts, cut into pieces
- 1 tbsp olive oil
- Salt and black pepper to season
- 6 large eggs
- 1 ½ cups water
- 2 tomatoes, seeded, chopped
- 6 tbsp Greek yogurt
- 1 head green lettuce, firm leaves removed for cups

Directions:

1. Preheat oven to 400ºF. Put the chicken pieces in a bowl, drizzle with olive oil, and sprinkle with salt and black pepper. Mix the ingredients until the chicken is well coated with the seasoning.

2. Put the chicken on a prepared baking sheet and spread out evenly. Slide the baking sheet in the oven and bake the chicken until cooked through and golden brown for 8 minutes, turning once.

3. Bring the eggs to boil in salted water in a pot over medium heat for 6 minutes. Run the eggs in cold water, peel, and chop into small pieces. Transfer to a salad bowl.

4. Remove the chicken from the oven when ready and add to the salad bowl. Include the tomatoes and Greek yogurt; mix evenly with a spoon. Layer two lettuce leaves each as cups and fill with two tablespoons of egg salad each. Serve with chilled blueberry juice.

Nutrition Info:

- Info Per Servings 4g Carbs, 21g Protein, 24.5g Fat, 325 Calories

Salsa Verde Chicken Soup

Servings: 4
Cooking Time: 15 Minutes
Ingredients:

- ½ cup salsa verde
- 2 cups cooked and shredded chicken
- 2 cups chicken broth
- 1 cup shredded cheddar cheese
- 4 ounces cream cheese
- ½ tsp chili powder
- ½ tsp ground cumin
- ½ tsp fresh cilantro, chopped
- Salt and black pepper, to taste

Directions:

1. Combine the cream cheese, salsa verde, and broth, in a food processor; pulse until smooth. Transfer the mixture to a pot and place over medium heat. Cook until hot, but do not bring to a boil.
2. Add chicken, chili powder, and cumin and cook for about 3-5 minutes, or until it is heated through.
3. Stir in Cheddar cheese and season with salt and pepper to taste. If it is very thick, add a few tablespoons of water and boil for 1-3 more minutes. Serve hot in bowls sprinkled with fresh cilantro.

Nutrition Info:

- Info Per Servings 3g Carbs, 25g Protein, 23g Fat, 346 Calories

Homemade Cold Gazpacho Soup

Servings: 6
Cooking Time: 15 Minutes
Ingredients:

- 2 small green peppers, roasted
- 2 large red peppers, roasted
- 2 medium avocados, flesh scoped out
- 2 garlic cloves
- 2 spring onions, chopped
- 1 cucumber, chopped
- 1 cup olive oil
- 2 tbsp lemon juice
- 4 tomatoes, chopped
- 7 ounces goat cheese
- 1 small red onion, chopped
- 2 tbsp apple cider vinegar
- Salt to taste

Directions:

1. Place the peppers, tomatoes, avocados, red onion, garlic, lemon juice, olive oil, vinegar, and salt, in a food processor. Pulse until your desired consistency is reached. Taste and adjust the seasoning.
2. Transfer the mixture to a pot. Stir in cucumber and spring onions. Cover and chill in the fridge at least 2 hours. Divide the soup between 6 bowls. Serve very cold, generously topped with goat cheese and an extra drizzle of olive oil.

Nutrition Info:

- Info Per Servings 6.5g Carbs, 7.5g Protein, 45.8g Fat, 528 Calories

Chicken And Cauliflower Rice Soup

Servings: 8

Cooking Time: 20 Mins

Ingredients:

- 2 cooked, boneless chicken breast halves, shredded
- 2 packages Steamed Cauliflower Rice
- 1/4 cup celery, chopped
- 1/2 cup onion, chopped
- 4 garlic cloves, minced
- Salt and ground black pepper to taste
- 2 teaspoons poultry seasoning
- 4 cups chicken broth
- ½ cup butter
- 2 cups heavy cream

Directions:

1. Heat butter in a large pot over medium heat, add onion, celery and garlic cloves to cook until tender. Meanwhile, place the riced cauliflower steam bags in the microwave following directions on the package.
2. Add the riced cauliflower, seasoning, salt and black pepper to butter mixture, saute them for 7 minutes on medium heat, stirring constantly to well combined.
3. Bring cooked chicken breast halves, broth and heavy cream to a broil. When it starts boiling, lower the heat, cover and simmer for 15 minutes.

Nutrition Info:

- Info Per Servings 6g Carbs, 27g Protein, 30g Fat, 415 Calories

Corn And Bacon Chowder

Servings: 8

Cooking Time: 23 Minutes

Ingredients:

- ½ cup bacon, fried and crumbled
- 1 package celery, onion, and bell pepper mix
- 2 cups full-fat milk
- ½ cup sharp cheddar cheese, grated
- 5 tablespoons butter
- Pepper and salt to taste
- 1 cup water

Directions:

1. In a heavy-bottomed pot, melt butter.
2. Saute the bacon and celery for 3 minutes.
3. Turn fire on to medium. Add remaining ingredients and cook for 20 minutes until thick.
4. Serve and enjoy with a sprinkle of crumbled bacon.

Nutrition Info:

- Info Per Servings 4.4g Carbs, 16.6g Protein, 13.6g Fat, 210.5 Calories

Sour Cream And Cucumbers

Servings: 8
Cooking Time: 0 Minutes

Ingredients:

- ½ cup sour cream
- 3 tablespoons white vinegar
- 4 medium cucumbers, sliced thinly
- 1 small sweet onion, sliced thinly
- Salt and pepper to taste
- 3 tablespoons olive oil

Directions:

1. In a bowl, whisk the sour cream and vinegar. Season with salt and pepper to taste. Whisk until well-combined.
2. Add in the cucumber and the rest of the ingredients.
3. Toss to coat.
4. Allow chilling before serving.

Nutrition Info:

- Info Per Servings 4.8g Carbs, 0.9g Protein, 8.3g Fat, 96 Calories

Balsamic Cucumber Salad

Servings: 6
Cooking Time: 0 Minutes

Ingredients:

- 1 large English cucumber, halved and sliced
- 1 cup grape tomatoes, halved
- 1 medium red onion, sliced thinly
- ¼ cup balsamic vinaigrette
- ¾ cup feta cheese
- Salt and pepper to taste
- ¼ cup olive oil

Directions:

1. Place all ingredients in a bowl.
2. Toss to coat everything with the dressing.
3. Allow chilling before serving.

Nutrition Info:

- Info Per Servings 9g Carbs, 4.8g Protein, 16.7g Fat, 253 Calories

Creamy Cauliflower Soup With Chorizo Sausage

Servings: 4
Cooking Time: 40 Minutes

Ingredients:

- 1 cauliflower head, chopped
- 1 turnip, chopped
- 3 tbsp butter
- 1 chorizo sausage, sliced
- 2 cups chicken broth
- 1 small onion, chopped
- 2 cups water
- Salt and black pepper, to taste

Directions:

1. Melt 2 tbsp. of the butter in a large pot over medium heat. Stir in onion and cook until soft and golden, about 3-4 minutes. Add cauliflower and turnip, and cook for another 5 minutes.

2. Pour the broth and water over. Bring to a boil, simmer covered, and cook for about 20 minutes until the vegetables are tender. Remove from heat. Melt the remaining butter in a skillet. Add the chorizo sausage and cook for 5 minutes until crispy. Puree the soup with a hand blender until smooth. Taste and adjust the seasonings. Serve the soup in deep bowls topped with the chorizo sausage.

Nutrition Info:

- Info Per Servings 5.7g Carbs, 10g Protein, 19.1g Fat, 251 Calories

Tuna Caprese Salad

Servings: 4

Cooking Time: 10 Minutes

Ingredients:

- 2 cans tuna chunks in water, drained
- 2 tomatoes, sliced
- 8 oz fresh mozzarella cheese, sliced
- 6 basil leaves
- ½ cup black olives, pitted and sliced
- 2 tbsp extra virgin olive oil
- ½ lemon, juiced

Directions:

1. Place the tuna in the center of a serving platter. Arrange the cheese and tomato slices around the tuna. Alternate a slice of tomato, cheese, and a basil leaf.

2. To finish, scatter the black olives over the top, drizzle with olive oil and lemon juice, and serve with grilled chicken breasts.

Nutrition Info:

- Info Per Servings 1g Carbs, 21g Protein, 31g Fat, 360 Calories

Crunchy And Salty Cucumber

Servings: 4

Cooking Time: 0 Minutes

Ingredients:

- 2 Persian cucumbers, sliced thinly
- 1 medium radish, trimmed and sliced thinly
- Juice from 1 lemon
- ½ cup parmesan cheese, shredded
- A dash of flaky sea salt
- A dash of ground black pepper
- 5 tablespoons olive oil

Directions:

1. Place all vegetables in a bowl.
2. Stir in the lemon juice and parmesan cheese.
3. Season with salt and pepper to taste
4. Add olive oil or salad oil.
5. Toss to mix everything.

Nutrition Info:

- Info Per Servings 4g Carbs, 3.7g Protein, 20g Fat, 209 Calories

Arugula Prawn Salad With Mayo Dressing

Servings: 4

Cooking Time: 15 Minutes

Ingredients:

- 4 cups baby arugula
- ½ cup garlic mayonnaise
- 3 tbsp olive oil
- 1 lb tiger prawns, peeled and deveined
- 1 tsp Dijon mustard
- Salt and chili pepper to season
- 2 tbsp lemon juice

Directions:

1. Add the mayonnaise, lemon juice and mustard in a small bowl. Mix until smooth and creamy. Heat 2 tbps of olive oil in a skillet over medium heat, add the prawns, season with salt, and chili pepper, and fry in the oil for 3 minutes on each side until prawns are pink. Set aside to a plate.

2. Place the arugula in a serving bowl and pour half of the dressing on the salad. Toss with 2 spoons until mixed, and add the remaining dressing. Divide salad into 4 plates and serve with prawns.

Nutrition Info:

- Info Per Servings 2g Carbs, 8g Protein, 20.3g Fat, 215 Calories

Insalata Caprese

Servings: 8
Cooking Time: 0 Minutes
Ingredients:

- 2 ½ pounds tomatoes, cut into 1-in pieces
- 8 ounces mozzarella cheese pearls
- ½ cup ripe olives, pitted
- ¼ cup fresh basil, sliced thinly
- Balsamic vinegar (optional)
- Salt and pepper to taste
- 3 tablespoons olive oil

Directions:

1. Place all ingredients in a bowl.
2. Season with salt and pepper to taste. Drizzle with balsamic vinegar if available.
3. Toss to coat.
4. Serve immediately.

Nutrition Info:

- Info Per Servings 7g Carbs, 6g Protein, 12g Fat, 160 Calories

Asparagus Niçoise Salad

Servings: 4
Cooking Time: 0 Minutes
Ingredients:

- 1-pound fresh asparagus, trimmed and blanched
- 2 ½ ounces white tuna in oil
- ½ cup pitted Greek olives, halved
- ½ cup zesty Italian salad dressing
- Salt and pepper to taste
- 3 tablespoons olive oil

Directions:

1. Place all ingredients in a bowl.
2. Toss to mix all ingredients.
3. Serve.

Nutrition Info:

- Info Per Servings 10g Carbs, 8g Protein, 20g Fat, 239 Calories

Chicken Creamy Soup

Servings: 4
Cooking Time: 15 Minutes
Ingredients:

- 2 cups cooked and shredded chicken
- 3 tbsp butter, melted
- 4 cups chicken broth
- 4 tbsp chopped cilantro
- ⅓ cup buffalo sauce
- ½ cup cream cheese
- Salt and black pepper, to taste

Directions:

1. Blend the butter, buffalo sauce, and cream cheese, in a food processor, until smooth. Transfer to a pot, add the chicken broth and heat until hot but do not bring to a boil. Stir in chicken, salt, black pepper and cook until heated through. When ready, remove to soup bowls and serve garnished with cilantro.

Nutrition Info:

- Info Per Servings 5g Carbs, 26.5g Protein, 29.5g Fat, 406 Calories

Bacon And Pea Salad

Servings: 6

Cooking Time: 5 Minutes

Ingredients:

- 4 bacon strips
- 2 cups fresh peas
- ½ cup shredded cheddar cheese
- ½ cup ranch salad dressing
- 1/3 cup chopped red onions
- Salt and pepper to taste
- 3 tablespoons olive oil

Directions:

1. Heat skillet over medium flame and fry the bacon until crispy or until the fat has rendered. Transfer into a plate lined with a paper towel and crumble.
2. In a bowl, combine the rest of the ingredients and toss to coat.
3. Add in the bacon bits last.

Nutrition Info:

- Info Per Servings 2.9g Carbs, 3.5g Protein, 20.4g Fat, 205 Calories

Broccoli Cheese Soup

Servings: 4

Cooking Time: 20 Minutes

Ingredients:

- ¾ cup heavy cream
- 1 onion, diced
- 1 tsp minced garlic
- 4 cups chopped broccoli
- 4 cups veggie broth
- 2 tbsp butter
- 2 ¾ cups grated cheddar cheese
- ¼ cup cheddar cheese to garnish
- Salt and black pepper, to taste
- ½ bunch fresh mint, chopped

Directions:

1. Melt the butter in a large pot over medium heat. Sauté onion and garlic for 3 minutes or until tender, stirring occasionally. Season with salt and pepper. Add the broth, broccoli and bring to a boil.
2. Reduce the heat and simmer for 10 minutes. Puree the soup with a hand blender until smooth. Add in the cheese and cook about 1 minute. Taste, season with salt and pepper. Stir in the heavy cream.Serve in bowls with the reserved grated Cheddar cheese and sprinkled with fresh mint.

Nutrition Info:

- Info Per Servings 7g Carbs, 23.8g Protein, 52.3g Fat, 561 Calories

Butternut And Kale Soup

Servings: 10
Cooking Time: 30 Minutes
Ingredients:

- 1 package Italian turkey sausage links, casings removed
- ½ medium butternut squash, peeled and cubed
- 2 cartons reduced-sodium chicken broth
- 1 bunch kale, trimmed and coarsely chopped
- 1/2 cup shaved Parmesan cheese
- 6 tablespoons butter
- Water
- Salt to taste

Directions:

1. In a stockpot, cook sausage over medium heat until no longer pink, breaking into crumbles, 8-10 minutes.
2. Add squash and broth; bring to a boil. Gradually stir in kale, allowing it to wilt slightly between additions. Return to a boil.
3. Reduce heat; simmer, uncovered, until vegetables are tender, 15-20 minutes. Top servings with cheese.

Nutrition Info:

- Info Per Servings 5.3g Carbs, 13g Protein, 5g Fat, 118 Calories

Minty Watermelon Cucumber

Servings: 12
Cooking Time: 0 Minutes
Ingredients:

- 8 cups cubed seedless watermelon
- 2 English cucumbers, halved and sliced
- ¼ cup minced fresh mint
- ¼ cup balsamic vinegar
- ¼ cup olive oil
- Salt and pepper to taste

Directions:

1. Place everything in a bowl and toss to coat everything.
2. Allow chilling before serving.

Nutrition Info:

- Info Per Servings 4g Carbs, 0.5g Protein, 8.1g Fat, 95 Calories

Coconut Cauliflower Soup

Servings: 10
Cooking Time: 26 Minutes
Ingredients:

- 1 medium onion, finely chopped
- 3 tablespoons yellow curry paste
- 2 medium heads cauliflower, broken into florets
- 1 carton vegetable broth
- 1 cup coconut milk
- 2 tablespoons olive oil

Directions:

1. In a large saucepan, heat oil over medium heat. Add onion; cook and stir until softened, 2-3 minutes.
2. Add curry paste; cook until fragrant, 1-2 minutes.
3. Add cauliflower and broth. Increase heat to high; bring to a boil. Reduce heat to medium-low; cook, covered, about 20 minutes.
4. Stir in coconut milk; cook an additional minute.
5. Remove from heat; cool slightly.
6. Puree in batches in a blender or food processor.
7. If desired, top with minced fresh cilantro.

Nutrition Info:

- Info Per Servings 10g Carbs, 3g Protein, 8g Fat, 111 Calories

Easy Tomato Salad

Servings: 4
Cooking Time: 0 Minutes
Ingredients:
- 1 ½ cups cherry tomatoes, sliced
- ¼ cup white wine vinegar
- 1/8 cup chives
- 3 tablespoons olive oil
- Salt and pepper to taste

Directions:
1. Put all ingredients in a bowl.
2. Toss to combine.
3. Serve immediately.

Nutrition Info:
- Info Per Servings 0.6g Carbs, 0.3g Protein, 10.1g Fat, 95 Calories

Bacon Tomato Salad

Servings: 6
Cooking Time: 0 Minutes
Ingredients:
- 6 ounces iceberg lettuce blend
- 2 cups grape tomatoes, halved
- ¾ cup coleslaw salad dressing
- ¾ cup cheddar cheese, shredded
- 12 bacon strips, cooked and crumbled
- Salt and pepper to taste

Directions:
1. Put the lettuce and tomatoes in a salad bowl.
2. Drizzle with the dressing and sprinkle with cheese. Season with salt and pepper to taste then mix.
3. Garnish with bacon bits on top.

Nutrition Info:
- Info Per Servings 8g Carbs, 10g Protein, 20g Fat, 268 Calories

Watermelon And Cucumber Salad

Servings: 10
Cooking Time: 0 Minutes
Ingredients:
- ½ large watermelon, diced
- 1 cucumber, peeled and diced
- 1 red onion, chopped
- ¼ cup feta cheese
- ½ cup heavy cream
- Salt to taste
- 5 tbsp MCT or coconut oil

Directions:
1. Place all ingredients in a bowl.
2. Toss everything to coat.
3. Place in the fridge to cool before serving.

Nutrition Info:
- Info Per Servings 2.5g Carbs, 0.9g Protein, 100g Fat, 910 Calories

Desserts And Drinks Recipes

Strawberry Yogurt Shake

Servings: 1

Cooking Time: 0 Minutes

Ingredients:

- ½ cup whole milk yogurt
- 4 strawberries, chopped
- 1 tbsp cocoa powder
- 3 tbsp coconut oil
- 1 tbsp pepitas
- 1 ½ cups water
- 1 packet Stevia, or more to taste

Directions:

1. Add all ingredients in a blender.
2. Blend until smooth and creamy.
3. Serve and enjoy.

Nutrition Info:

- Info Per Servings 10.5g Carbs, 7.7g Protein, 49.3g Fat, 496 Calories

Vanilla Bean Frappuccino

Servings: 4

Cooking Time: 6 Minutes

Ingredients:

- 3 cups unsweetened vanilla almond milk, chilled
- 2 tsp swerve
- 1 ½ cups heavy cream, cold
- 1 vanilla bean
- ¼ tsp xanthan gum
- Unsweetened chocolate shavings to garnish

Directions:

1. Combine the almond milk, swerve, heavy cream, vanilla bean, and xanthan gum in the blender, and process on high speed for 1 minute until smooth. Pour into tall shake glasses, sprinkle with chocolate shavings, and serve immediately.

Nutrition Info:

- Info Per Servings 6g Carbs, 15g Protein, 14g Fat, 193 Calories

Nutritiously Green Milk Shake

Servings: 1

Cooking Time: 5 Minutes

Ingredients:

- 1 cup coconut cream
- 1 packet Stevia, or more to taste
- 1 tbsp coconut flakes, unsweetened
- 2 cups spring mix salad
- 3 tbsps coconut oil
- 1 cup water

Directions:

1. Add all ingredients in a blender.
2. Blend until smooth and creamy.
3. Serve and enjoy.

Nutrition Info:

- Info Per Servings 10g Carbs, 10.5g Protein, 95.3g Fat, 887 Calories

Vanilla Flan With Mint

Servings: 4
Cooking Time: 10 Minutes
Ingredients:

- ⅓ cup erythritol, for caramel
- 2 cups almond milk
- 4 eggs
- 1 tbsp vanilla
- 1 tbsp lemon zest
- ½ cup erythritol, for custard
- 2 cup heavy whipping cream
- Mint leaves, to serve

Directions:

1. Heat the erythritol for the caramel in a deep pan. Add 2-3 tablespoons of water, and bring to a boil. Reduce the heat and cook until the caramel turns golden brown. Divide between 4-6 metal tins. Set aside and let them cool.

2. In a bowl, mix the eggs, remaining erythritol, lemon zest, and vanilla. Add the almond milk and beat again until well combined.

3. Pour the custard into each caramel-lined ramekin and place them into a deep baking tin. Fill over the way with the remaining hot water. Bake at 345 °F for 45-50 minutes. Using tongs, take out the ramekins and let them cool for at least 4 hours in the fridge. Run a knife slowly around the edges to invert onto a dish. Serve with dollops of whipped cream, scattered with mint leaves.

Nutrition Info:

- Info Per Servings 1.7g Carbs, 7.6g Protein, 26g Fat, 269 Calories

Granny Smith Apple Tart

Servings: 8
Cooking Time: 65 Minutes
Ingredients:

- 6 tbsp butter
- 2 cups almond flour
- 1 tsp cinnamon
- ⅓ cup sweetener
- Filling:
- 2 cups sliced Granny Smith
- ¼ cup butter
- ¼ cup sweetener
- ½ tsp cinnamon
- ½ tsp lemon juice
- Topping:
- ¼ tsp cinnamon
- 2 tbsp sweetener

Directions:

1. Preheat your oven to 370ºF and combine all crust ingredients in a bowl. Press this mixture into the bottom of a greased pan. Bake for 5 minutes.

2. Meanwhile, combine the apples and lemon juice in a bowl and let them sit until the crust is ready. Arrange them on top of the crust. Combine the rest of the filling ingredients, and brush this mixture over the apples. Bake for about 30 minutes.

3. Press the apples down with a spatula, return to oven, and bake for 20 more minutes. Combine the cinnamon and sweetener, in a bowl, and sprinkle over the tart.

4. Note: Granny Smith apples have just 9.5g of net carbs per 100g. Still high for you? Substitute with Chayote squash, which has the same texture and rich nutrients, and just around 4g of net carbs .

Nutrition Info:

- Info Per Servings 6.7g Carbs, 7g Protein, 26g Fat, 302 Calories

Coconut-melon Yogurt Shake

Servings: 1
Cooking Time: 0 Minutes
Ingredients:

- ¼ cup half and half
- 3 tbsp coconut oil
- ½ cup melon, slices
- 1 tbsp coconut flakes, unsweetened
- 1 tbsp chia seeds
- 1 ½ cups water
- 1 packet Stevia, or more to taste

Directions:

1. Add all ingredients in a blender.
2. Blend until smooth and creamy.
3. Serve and enjoy.

Nutrition Info:

- Info Per Servings 8g Carbs, 2.4g Protein, 43g Fat, 440 Calories

Boysenberry And Greens Shake

Servings: 1
Cooking Time: 0 Minutes
Ingredients:

- ¼ cup coconut milk
- 2 tbsps Boysenberry
- 2 packets Stevia, or as needed
- ¼ cup Baby Kale salad mix
- 3 tbsps MCT oil
- 1 ½ cups water

Directions:

1. Add all ingredients in a blender.
2. Blend until smooth and creamy.
3. Serve and enjoy.

Nutrition Info:

- Info Per Servings 3.9g Carbs, 1.7g Protein, 55.1g Fat, 502 Calories

No Nuts Fudge

Servings: 15
Cooking Time: 4 Hours
Ingredients:

- ¼ cup cocoa powder
- ½ teaspoon baking powder
- 1 stick of butter, melted
- 4 tablespoons erythritol
- 6 eggs, beaten
- Salt to taste.

Directions:

1. Mix all ingredients in a slow cooker.
2. Add a pinch of salt.
3. Mix until well combined.
4. Cover pot.
5. Press the low settings and adjust the time to 4 hours.

Nutrition Info:

- Info Per Servings 1.3g Carbs, 4.3g Protein, 12.2g Fat, 132 Calories

Brownies With Coco Milk

Servings: 10
Cooking Time: 6 Hours

Ingredients:

- ¾ cup coconut milk
- 1 teaspoon erythritol
- 2 tablespoons butter, melted
- 4 egg yolks, beaten
- 5 tablespoons cacao powder

Directions:

1. In a bowl, mix well all ingredients.
2. Lightly grease your slow cooker with cooking spray and pour in batter.
3. Cover and cook on low for six hours.
4. Serve and enjoy.

Nutrition Info:

- Info Per Servings 1.2g Carbs, 1.5g Protein, 8.4g Fat, 86 Calories

Eggless Strawberry Mousse

Servings: 6
Cooking Time: 6 Minutes + Cooling Time

Ingredients:

- 2 cups chilled heavy cream
- 2 cups fresh strawberries, hulled
- 5 tbsp erythritol
- 2 tbsp lemon juice
- ¼ tsp strawberry extract
- 2 tbsp sugar-free strawberry preserves

Directions:

1. Beat the heavy cream, in a bowl, with a hand mixer at high speed until a stiff peak forms, for about 1 minute; refrigerate immediately. Puree the strawberries in a blender and pour into a saucepan.
2. Add erythritol and lemon juice, and cook on low heat for 3 minutes while stirring continuously. Stir in the strawberry extract evenly, turn off heat and allow cooling. Fold in the whipped cream until evenly incorporated, and spoon into six ramekins. Refrigerate for 4 hours to solidify.
3. Garnish with strawberry preserves and serve immediately.

Nutrition Info:

- Info Per Servings 5g Carbs, 5g Protein, 24g Fat, 290 Calories

Coffee Fat Bombs

Servings: 6
Cooking Time: 3 Minutes + Cooling Time

Ingredients:

- 1 ½ cups mascarpone cheese
- ½ cup melted butter
- 3 tbsp unsweetened cocoa powder
- ¼ cup erythritol
- 6 tbsp brewed coffee, room temperature

Directions:

1. Whisk the mascarpone cheese, butter, cocoa powder, erythritol, and coffee with a hand mixer until creamy and fluffy, for 1 minute. Fill into muffin tins and freeze for 3 hours until firm.

Nutrition Info:

- Info Per Servings 2g Carbs, 4g Protein, 14g Fat, 145 Calories

Green Tea Brownies With Macadamia Nuts

Servings: 4

Cooking Time: 28 Minutes

Ingredients:

- 1 tbsp green tea powder
- ¼ cup unsalted butter, melted
- 4 tbsp swerve confectioner's sugar
- A pinch of salt
- ¼ cup coconut flour
- ½ tsp low carb baking powder
- 1 egg
- ¼ cup chopped macadamia nuts

Directions:

1. Preheat the oven to 350ºF and line a square baking dish with parchment paper. Pour the melted butter into a bowl, add sugar and salt, and whisk to combine. Crack the egg into the bowl.
2. Beat the mixture until the egg has incorporated. Pour the coconut flour, green tea, and baking powder into a fine-mesh sieve and sift them into the egg bowl; stir. Add the nuts, stir again, and pour the mixture into the lined baking dish. Bake for 18 minutes, remove and slice into brownie cubes. Serve warm.

Nutrition Info:

- Info Per Servings 2.2g Carbs, 5.2g Protein, 23.1g Fat, 248 Calories

Lemon Gummies

Servings: 4

Cooking Time: 15 Minutes

Ingredients:

- 1/4 cup fresh lemon juice
- 2 Tablespoons gelatin powder
- 2 Tablespoons stevia, to taste
- ½ cup half and half
- 1 Tablespoon water

Directions:

1. In a small saucepan, heat up water and lemon juice.
2. Slowly stir in the gelatin powder and the rest of the ingredients. Heating and mixing well until dissolved.
3. Pour into silicone molds.
4. Freeze or refrigerate for 2+ hours until firm.

Nutrition Info:

- Info Per Servings 1.0g Carbs, 3.0g Protein, 7g Fat, 88 Calories

Spicy Cheese Crackers

Servings: 4
Cooking Time: 10 Mins
Ingredients:

- 3/4 cup almond flour
- 1 egg
- 2 tablespoons cream cheese
- 2 cups shredded Parmesan cheese
- 1/2 teaspoon red pepper flakes
- 1 tablespoon dry ranch salad dressing mix

Directions:

1. Preheat oven to 425 degrees F.
2. Combine Parmesan and cream cheese in a microwave safe bowl and microwave in 30 second intervals. Add the cheese to mix well, and whisk along the almond flour, egg, ranch seasoning, and red pepper flakes, stirring occasionally.
3. Transfer the dough in between two parchment-lined baking sheets. Form the dough into rolls by cutting off plum-sized pieces of dough with dough cutter into 1-inch square pieces, yielding about 60 pieces.
4. Place crackers to a baking sheet lined parchment. Bake for 5 minutes, flipping halfway, then continue to bake for 5 minutes more. Chill before serving.

Nutrition Info:

- Info Per Servings 18g Carbs, 17g Protein, 4g Fat, 235 Calories

Coco-loco Creamy Shake

Servings: 1
Cooking Time: 0 Minutes
Ingredients:

- ½ cup coconut milk
- 2 tbsp Dutch-processed cocoa powder, unsweetened
- 1 cup brewed coffee, chilled
- 1 tbsp hemp seeds
- 1-2 packets Stevia
- 3 tbsps MCT oil or coconut oil

Directions:

1. Add all ingredients in a blender.
2. Blend until smooth and creamy.
3. Serve and enjoy.

Nutrition Info:

- Info Per Servings 10.2g Carbs, 5.4g Protein, 61.1g Fat, 567 Calories

Green And Fruity Smoothie

Servings: 2
Cooking Time: 0 Minutes
Ingredients:

- 1 cup spinach, packed
- ½ cup strawberries, chopped
- ½ avocado, peeled, pitted, and frozen
- 1 tbsp almond butter
- ¼ cup packed kale, stem discarded, and leaves chopped
- 1 cup ice-cold water
- 5 tablespoons MCT oil or coconut oil

Directions:

1. Blend all ingredients in a blender until smooth and creamy.
2. Serve and enjoy.

Nutrition Info:

- Info Per Servings 10g Carbs, 1.6g Protein, 47.3g Fat, 459 Calories

Almond Milk Hot Chocolate

Servings: 4
Cooking Time: 7 Minutes
Ingredients:
- 3 cups almond milk
- 4 tbsp unsweetened cocoa powder
- 2 tbsp swerve
- 3 tbsp almond butter
- Finely chopped almonds to garnish

Directions:
1. In a saucepan, add the almond milk, cocoa powder, and swerve. Stir the mixture until the sugar dissolves. Set the pan over low to heat through for 5 minutes, without boiling.
2. Swirl the mix occasionally. Turn the heat off and stir in the almond butter to be incorporated. Pour the hot chocolate into mugs and sprinkle with chopped almonds. Serve warm.

Nutrition Info:
- Info Per Servings 0.6g Carbs, 4.5g Protein, 21.5g Fat, 225 Calories

Coconut Milk Pudding

Servings: 2
Cooking Time: 5 Minutes
Ingredients:
- ½ teaspoon vanilla extract
- 1 cup coconut milk
- 1 tablespoon gelatin, unsweetened
- 2 teaspoons erythritol
- 3 egg yolks, beaten
- 4 tablespoons MCT or coconut oil

Directions:
1. Add all ingredients in a pot.
2. Bring to a simmer, mix continuously, and cook for 3 minutes.
3. Transfer to a bowl and refrigerate for an hour.
4. Serve and enjoy.

Nutrition Info:
- Info Per Servings 9.2g Carbs, 8.3g Protein, 49.7g Fat, 529 Calories

Blackberry Cheese Vanilla Blocks

Servings: 5
Cooking Time: 20mins
Ingredients:
- ½ cup blackberries
- 6 eggs
- 4 oz mascarpone cheese
- 1 tsp vanilla extract
- 4 tbsp stevia
- 8 oz melted coconut oil
- ½ tsp baking powder

Directions:
1. Except for blackberries, blend all ingredients in a blender until smooth.
2. Combine blackberries with blended mixture and transfer to a baking dish.
3. Bake blackberries mixture in the oven at 320°F for 20 minutes. Serve.

Nutrition Info:
- Info Per Servings 15g Carbs, 13g Protein, 4g Fat, 199 Calories

Choco Coffee Milk Shake

Servings: 1
Cooking Time: 0 Minutes
Ingredients:

- ½ cup coconut milk
- 1 tbsp cocoa powder
- 1 cup brewed coffee, chilled
- 1 packet Stevia, or more to taste
- ½ tsp cinnamon
- 5 tbsps coconut oil

Directions:

1. Add all ingredients in a blender.
2. Blend until smooth and creamy.
3. Serve and enjoy.

Nutrition Info:

- Info Per Servings 10g Carbs, 4.1g Protein, 97.4g Fat, 880 Calories

Creamy Choco Shake

Servings: 1
Cooking Time: 0 Minutes
Ingredients:

- ½ cup heavy cream
- 2 tbsp cocoa powder
- 1 packet Stevia, or more to taste
- 1 cup water
- 3 tbsps coconut oil

Directions:

1. Add all ingredients in a blender.
2. Blend until smooth and creamy.
3. Serve and enjoy.

Nutrition Info:

- Info Per Servings 7.9g Carbs, 3.2g Protein, 64.6g Fat, 582 Calories

Crispy Zucchini Chips

Servings: 5
Cooking Time: 20 Mins
Ingredients:

- 1 large egg, beaten
- 1 cup. almond flour
- 1 medium zucchini, thinly sliced
- 3/4 cup Parmesan cheese, grated
- Cooking spray

Directions:

1. Preheat oven to 400 degrees F. Line a baking pan with parchment paper.
2. In a bowl, mix together Parmesan cheese and almond flour.
3. In another bowl whisk the egg. Dip each zucchini slice in the egg, then the cheese mixture until finely coated.
4. Spray zucchini slices with cooking spray and place in the prepared oven.
5. Bake for 20 minutes until crispy. Serve.

Nutrition Info:

- Info Per Servings 16.8g Carbs, 10.8g Protein, 6g Fat, 215.2 Calories

Cardamom-cinnamon Spiced Coco-latte

Servings: 1
Cooking Time: 0 Minutes
Ingredients:

- ½ cup coconut milk
- ¼ tsp cardamom powder
- 1 tbsp chocolate powder
- 1 ½ cups brewed coffee, chilled
- 1 tbsp coconut oil
- ¼ tsp cinnamon
- ¼ tsp nutmeg

Directions:

1. Add all ingredients in a blender.
2. Blend until smooth and creamy.
3. Serve and enjoy.

Nutrition Info:

- Info Per Servings 7.5g Carbs, 3.8g Protein, 38.7g Fat, 362 Calories

Nutty Arugula Yogurt Smoothie

Servings: 1
Cooking Time: 0 Minutes
Ingredients:

- 1 cup whole milk yogurt
- 1 cup baby arugula
- 3 tbsps avocado oil
- 2 tbsps macadamia nuts
- 1 packet Stevia, or more to taste
- 1 cup water

Directions:

1. Add all ingredients in a blender.
2. Blend until smooth and creamy.
3. Serve and enjoy.

Nutrition Info:

- Info Per Servings 9.4g Carbs, 9.3g Protein, 51.5g Fat, 540 Calories

Chocolate Cakes

Servings: 6
Cooking Time: 25 Minutes
Ingredients:

- ½ cup almond flour
- ¼ cup xylitol
- 1 tsp baking powder
- ½ tsp baking soda
- 1 tsp cinnamon, ground
- A pinch of salt
- A pinch of ground cloves
- ½ cup butter, melted
- ½ cup buttermilk
- 1 egg
- 1 tsp pure almond extract
- For the Frosting:
- 1 cup double cream
- 1 cup dark chocolate, flaked

Directions:

1. Preheat the oven to 360°F. Use a cooking spray to grease a donut pan.
2. In a bowl, mix the cloves, almond flour, baking powder, salt, baking soda, xylitol, and cinnamon. In a separate bowl, combine the almond extract, butter, egg, buttermilk, and cream. Mix the wet mixture into the dry mixture. Evenly ladle the batter into the donut pan. Bake for 17 minutes.
3. Set a pan over medium heat and warm double cream; simmer for 2 minutes. Fold in the chocolate flakes; combine until all the chocolate melts; let cool. Spread the top of the cakes with the frosting.

Nutrition Info:

- Info Per Servings 10g Carbs, 4.8g Protein, 20g Fat, 218 Calories

Cranberry White Chocolate Barks

Servings: 6
Cooking Time: 5 Minutes
Ingredients:

- 10 oz unsweetened white chocolate, chopped
- ½ cup erythritol
- ⅓ cup dried cranberries, chopped
- ⅓ cup toasted walnuts, chopped
- ¼ tsp pink salt

Directions:

1. Line a baking sheet with parchment paper. Pour chocolate and erythritol in a bowl, and melt in the microwave for 25 seconds, stirring three times until fully melted. Stir in the cranberries, walnuts, and salt, reserving a few cranberries and walnuts for garnishing.
2. Pour the mixture on the baking sheet and spread out. Sprinkle with remaining cranberries and walnuts. Refrigerate for 2 hours to set. Break into bite-size pieces to serve.

Nutrition Info:

- Info Per Servings 3g Carbs, 6g Protein, 21g Fat, 225 Calories

Appendix : Recipes Index

A

Alaskan Cod With Mustard Cream Sauce 44
Almond Milk Hot Chocolate 78
Angel Hair Shirataki With Creamy Shrimp 48
Arugula Prawn Salad With Mayo Dressing 67
Asparagus Niçoise Salad 68
Avocado And Salmon 45
Avocado Tuna Boats 50

B

Baba Ganoush Eggplant Dip 7
Bacon And Chicken Cottage Pie 26
Bacon And Pea Salad 69
Bacon Stew With Cauliflower 39
Bacon Tomato Salad 71
Bacon Wrapped Salmon 44
Bacon-flavored Kale Chips 16
Baked Fish With Feta And Tomato 40
Baked Salmon With Pistachio Crust 42
Balsamic Brussels Sprouts With Prosciutto 7
Balsamic Cucumber Salad 66
Balsamic Zucchini 15
Beef And Ale Pot Roast 36
Beef Brisket In Mustard Sauce 29
Beef Enchilada Stew 38
Beef Italian Sandwiches 31
Beef Steak Filipino Style 39
Beef Stovies 30
Bell Pepper Stuffed Avocado 55
Blackberry Cheese Vanilla Blocks 78
Blackened Fish Tacos With Slaw 41
Boysenberry And Greens Shake 74
Broccoli Cheese Soup 69
Broccoli Slaw Salad With Mustard-mayo Dressing 62
Brownies With Coco Milk 75
Brussels Sprouts With Tofu 53
Butternut And Kale Soup 70
Buttery Herb Roasted Radishes 6

C

Cardamom-cinnamon Spiced Coco-latte 80
Cauliflower & Hazelnut Salad 52

Cauliflower & Mushrooms Stuffed Peppers 59
Cauliflower Fritters 51
Cauliflower Gouda Casserole 61
Cauliflower Mash 57
Cedar Salmon With Green Onion 47
Chard Swiss Dip 56
Cheese Stuffed Chicken Breasts With Spinach 28
Cheesy Cauliflower Falafel 58
Cheesy Chicken Fritters With Dill Dip 8
Chicken And Cauliflower Rice Soup 65
Chicken And Spinach 27
Chicken Breasts With Cheddar & Pepperoni 24
Chicken Cabbage Soup 62
Chicken Country Style 19
Chicken Creamy Soup 68
Chicken Curry 21
Chicken Gumbo 25
Chicken Thighs With Broccoli & Green Onions 18
Chicken With Monterey Jack Cheese 24
Chili Lime Chicken 20
Chili Turkey Patties With Cucumber Salsa 20
Choco Coffee Milk Shake 79
Chocolate Cakes 81
Citrusy Brussels Sprouts Salad 62
Cobb Egg Salad In Lettuce Cups 63
Coco-loco Creamy Shake 77
Coconut And Chocolate Bars 12
Coconut Cauliflower Soup 70
Coconut Milk Pudding 78
Coconut Milk Sauce Over Crabs 45
Coconut-melon Yogurt Shake 74
Cod With Balsamic Tomatoes 49
Coffee Fat Bombs 75
Corn And Bacon Chowder 65
Cranberry White Chocolate Barks 81
Creamy Cauliflower Soup With Chorizo Sausage 66
Creamy Choco Shake 79
Creamy Cucumber Avocado Soup 51
Crispy Keto Pork Bites 11
Crispy Zucchini Chips 79
Crunchy And Salty Cucumber 67

D

Devilled Eggs With Sriracha Mayo 16

E

Easy Asian Chicken 20
Easy Tomato Salad 71

Egg And Tomato Salad 53
Eggless Strawberry Mousse 75
Enchilada Sauce On Mahi Mahi 44

F

Flounder With Dill And Capers 46
Fried Chicken With Coconut Sauce 19

G

Garlic Flavored Kale Taters 13
Garlic Lemon Mushrooms 56
Golden Pompano In Microwave 42
Granny Smith Apple Tart 73
Grated Cauliflower With Seasoned Mayo 58
Green And Fruity Smoothie 77
Green Tea Brownies With Macadamia Nuts 76
Grilled Cauliflower 54
Grilled Cheese The Keto Way 57
Grilled Pork Loin Chops With Barbecue Sauce 35
Grilled Spicy Eggplant 55
Ground Beef And Cabbage Stir Fry 33
Guacamole 55

H

Homemade Cold Gazpacho Soup 64

I

Insalata Caprese 68

J

Jalapeno Popper Spread 6
Jamaican Pork Oven Roast 38

L

Lemon Gummies 76
Lemon Marinated Salmon With Spices 41
Lemon Pork Chops With Buttered Brussels Sprouts 32
Lemon-rosemary Shrimps 40
Lemony Fried Artichokes 6

M

Mexican Soup 63
Minty Watermelon Cucumber 70

Morning Coconut Smoothie 57
Morning Granola 60
Mozzarella & Prosciutto Wraps 10
Mushroom Pork Chops 37
Mustardy Pork Chops 30

N

No Nuts Fudge 74
Nutritiously Green Milk Shake 72
Nutty Arugula Yogurt Smoothie 80
Nutty Avocado Crostini With Nori 15

O

Onion Cheese Muffins 13
Oregano & Chili Flattened Chicken 21

P

Pancetta & Chicken Casserole 28
Pancetta Sausage With Kale 34
Paprika 'n Cajun Seasoned Onion Rings 60
Parmesan Crackers 8
Parsley Beef Burgers 35
Party Bacon And Pistachio Balls 9
Peanut Butter Pork Stir-fry 29
Pesto Chicken 17
Pesto Stuffed Mushrooms 11
Pork Chops And Peppers 39
Pork Lettuce Cups 33
Pulled Pork With Avocado 37
Pumpkin Bake 56

R

Red Curry Halibut 50
Reese Cups 13
Roast Chicken With Herb Stuffing 23
Roasted Asparagus With Spicy Eggplant Dip 59
Roasted Chicken Breasts With Capers 22
Roasted Chicken With Herbs 19
Roasted Chicken With Tarragon 25
Roasted Spicy Beef 34
Roasted String Beans, Mushrooms & Tomato Plate 10

S

Salmon Panzanella 47
Salsa Verde Chicken Soup 64

Seasoned Salmon With Parmesan 45
Shrimp In Curry Sauce 46
Shrimp Spread 43
Simple Beef Curry 31
Simple Chicken Garlic-tomato Stew 27
Simple Corned Beef 32
Simple Tender Crisp Cauli-bites 9
Slow Cooker Pork 37
Smoked Mackerel Patties 48
Smoky Paprika Chicken 23
Sour Cream And Cucumbers 66
Spiced Pork Roast With Collard Greens 38
Spicy Cheese Crackers 77
Spicy Devilled Eggs With Herbs 9
Spinach And Ricotta Gnocchi 14
Steamed Chili-rubbed Tilapia 40
Steamed Cod With Ginger 43
Steamed Ginger Scallion Fish 49
Strawberry Mug Cake 53
Strawberry Yogurt Shake 72
Stuffed Jalapeno 10
Sweet Garlic Chicken Skewers 18

T

Tart Raspberry Crumble Bar 12
Teriyaki Chicken Wings 14
Thyme Chicken Thighs 22
Thyme-sesame Crusted Halibut 49
Tofu Sesame Skewers With Warm Kale Salad 54
Tuna Caprese Salad 67
Turkey Enchilada Bowl 26
Turkey, Coconut And Kale Chili 17

V

Vanilla Bean Frappuccino 72
Vanilla Flan With Mint 73
Vegetable Tempeh Kabobs 52

W

Watermelon And Cucumber Salad 71
White Wine Lamb Chops 33

Z

Zoodle, Bacon, Spinach, And Halloumi Gratin 36
Zoodles With Avocado & Olives 61

Printed in Great Britain
by Amazon

29097424R00057